THERE ARE NO SIMPLE RULES FOR DATING MY DAUGHTER!

Also from the Boys Town Press

No Room for Bullies

Changing Children's Behavior by Changing the People, Places, and Activities in Their Lives

Who's Raising Your Child?

Good Night, Sweet Dreams, I Love You, Now Get into Bed and Go to Sleep

Common Sense Parenting®

Common Sense Parenting of Toddlers and Preschoolers

Common Sense Parenting Learn-at-Home Video or DVD Kit

Parenting to Build Character in Your Teen

Fathers, Come Home

Angry Kids, Frustrated Parents

Dealing with Your Kids' 7 Biggest Troubles

Practical Tools for Foster Parents

DVDs For Parents

Common Sense Parenting®
Vol. 1: Building Relationships
Vol. 2: Teaching Children Self-Control

For Adolescents

Little Sisters, Listen Up!

Guys, Let's Keep It Real!

Boundaries: A Guide for Teens

A Good Friend

Who's in the Mirror?

What's Right for Me?

For a free Boys Town Press catalog, call 1-800-282-6657.
Visit our Web site at www.boystownpress.org

Girls and Boys Town National Hotline 1-800-448-3000
Parents and kids can call toll-free, anytime, with any problem.

THERE ARE NO SIMPLE RULES FOR DATING MY DAUGHTER!

Surviving the
Pitfalls and Pratfalls
of Teen Relationships

Laura J. Buddenberg and Kathleen M. McGee

BOYS TOWN, NEBRASKA

There Are No Simple Rules For Dating My Daughter

Published by the Boys Town Press
Boys Town, Nebraska 68010

The Boys Town Press is the publishing division of Girls and Boys Town, the original Father Flanagan's Boys' Home.

Publisher's Cataloging in Publication

Buddenberg, Laura J.

There are no simple rules for dating my daughter! : surviving the pitfalls and pratfalls of teen relationships / by Laura J. Buddenberg and Kathleen M. McGee. -- 1st ed. -- Boys Town, Neb. : Boys Town Press, c2006.

    p. ; cm.

    ISBN-13: 978-1-889322-71-1 (pbk.)
    ISBN-10: 1-889322-71-7 (pbk.)
    Includes bibliographical references.

    1. Dating (Social customs) 2. Interpersonal relations in adolescence. 3. Interpersonal attraction. 4. Teenage girls--Conduct of life. 5. Teenage girls--Psychology. 6. Teenage boys. 7. Parenting. 8. Parent and teenager. I. McGee, Kathleen M. II. Title.

HQ801 .B83 2006
646.77/083520608

10 9 8 7 6 5 4 3 2 1

Acknowledgments

We want to extend our deepest appreciation to the many wonderful young ladies and families we have met, worked with, and learned from over the years. Thank you for welcoming us into your lives and sharing with us your hopes, dreams, struggles, and triumphs. You continue to inspire us.

A special thank you also to Father Val Peter, for his professional guidance and support; to our editors, Stan Graeve, Terry Hyland, and Barbara Lonnborg, for helping us prepare this manuscript; and to our graphic artist, Eli Hernandez.

To our families...

I want to express my thanks to my two beautiful daughters, Cate and Claire; my husband, Roger (I wouldn't want to be on this wild parenting ride with anyone else!); and my parents, Morgan and Judy Holmes. – *Laura*

All my love and gratitude to my husband, Chris, son, Jack, and my parents, Kurt and Jean Sorensen. – *Kathleen*

Table of Contents

Introduction

"But Mom, we're in love!"

"I'm 13! Why can't I date? All my friends are!"

"It's a date. You gotta let me stay out past midnight!"

Are you a parent who is agonizing over the fact that your daughter seems obsessed with the opposite sex? Are you asking yourself, how can this be happening already? After all, you think, it wasn't that long ago that she was climbing into your lap, anxiously waiting for you to brush and braid her hair. Now, the only place she sits anxiously is in front of her computer, waiting for yet another IM (instant message) from a BF (boyfriend). Where did that sweet creature go who gazed at you with eyes that said you were the single most important person in her life? When did your "baby girl" go from the innocence of playing dolls and dress up to the more adult pursuit of eyeing guys and obsessing over dates?

Parents' reactions to, and acceptance of, their daughters' growing maturity and interests vary. Some feel pure dread, as expressed in this comment from one only-half-joking father: "My daughter can date when she's 40 or after I'm dead – whichever comes first!" Others experience uncertainty. They realize today's youth culture is far different from the one they experienced decades ago. For these parents, they struggle with a more fundamental question: "What is the right age for my daughter to start dating?" There are still other parents who seem ambivalent. When their 10-, 11-, or 12-year-old blurts out "I have a boyfriend," they chuckle and say, "How cute," and never give it a second thought.

While parents try to understand the infatuations, crushes, and courtships that are part of an adolescent's life, their kids entertain more immediate concerns, such as "How can I make a guy go out with me?" or "How much money does it take to have a great date?"

> "Nothing spoils the taste of peanut butter like unrequited love."
>
> – CHARLIE BROWN
> (FROM PEANUTS
> COMIC STRIP)

When we talk with parents and teens, we hear a lot of chatter about dating and relationships. Parents ask about rules. Boys ask about what girls want. Girls ask about what boys want. You would think with all the questions, families would be sitting down and talking about an issue that's as natural and predictable in adolescence as pimples and peer pressure. But many don't. Maybe it's because Mom and Dad never had dating rules while growing up, and they survived. Maybe it's because parents equate dating with sex – an assumption that too often results in thunderous silence. Maybe it's the child. Maybe she is too embarrassed to approach her parents. Maybe she's ashamed of her relationship or afraid to reveal just how intimate the relationship has become. Whatever the reasons, there is often very little conversation and lots of confusion.

As authors of this book, we want to help you start a dialogue in your family. We want to chip away the apprehension, fear, denial, or indifference that we've seen paralyze parents, leaving their teens entangled in dating relationships that have no purpose or direction. A lack of good information and good communication seems to be the biggest problem. Young people tell us they can't talk to their parents. So instead, they seek advice from friends, some of whom are involved in relationships that appear as unhealthy as those that populate the "reality" TV programs – *The Real World, Laguna Beach,* etc. – teens tune into every week. As parents, we understand this can be a terribly sensitive time as you have to admit your child is growing up. But rather than turn this whole area of your child's life over to her friends or random messages from pop culture, why not offer your own voice of support and guidance?

As the title of our book suggests, our focus is on the female side of the boy/girl equation. However, the activities and information we've included are good for the whole family, including your sons. The reason we're zeroing in on girls is because, as women, we're acutely aware of the unique external pressures and internal desires that girls grapple with from early adolescence through early adulthood. Also, parents, especially dads, seem more concerned about their daughters. After all, girls tend to become interested in opposite-gender relationships at an earlier age than the boys they have crushes on. This is partly explained by the fact that girls mature – both physically and cognitively – faster than boys. Their communication skills develop at an earlier age, too. You are more likely to hear your daughters chatting and dreaming about finding their Prince Charming long before sons (of a similar age) start looking at girls as dazzling damsels they'd like to date.

For us, examining the role girls play in dating relationships is a logical place to start. Girls and women are often the gatekeepers in relationships. They set the bar for how they want to be treated, and most of the time, guys will treat girls the way girls let them. (Adolescent boys admit that to us all the time.) In other words, if girls allow guys to call them demeaning names, such as "bitch" or "ho," and to take advantage of them physically, financially, or emotionally, they attract guys who will do just that. The girls become objects,

> "Friendship often ends in love; but love in friendship, never."
>
> – Charles Caleb Colton
> British Clergyman
> and Author

not individuals. This type of guy, usually referred to as a "player," uses girls for selfish reasons, be it social status or sexual favors. On the other hand, when girls demand to be treated with respect – physical, verbal, and emotional – they attract the type of guys who are sincerely interested in relationships based on friendships. We want to help you help your daughter become a girl who demands such respect.

Who We Are

When boys in junior and senior high school tell us they often follow the social cues of their girlfriends, we know that the girls are able to shape their relationships so they don't get hurt. We've learned a lot from the teens and families we've met through both our personal and professional experiences. Laura has two teenage daughters.

Kathie, the mother of a toddler, is a former high school teacher and creator of a relationship education curriculum. Together, we have worked with youth and families at Girls and Boys Town for more than two decades. As professional trainers, we have presented workshops and given talks on a wide range of social and cultural issues, including sexual harassment, cyberbullying, and personal boundaries. Our audiences include children, teens, parents, educators, and others who care about and for youth. We've been fortunate to work with young people in school systems, interacting with them and learning about the personal relationships they had, have, and hope for. They've shared with us – two complete strangers – their wishes, fears, desires, and frustrations. What they've taught us is that our kids really do want to be in relationships that are not complicated by what their peers or pop culture defines as "ideal." That's good news for parents.

How to Use This Book

Whether you're just now starting to hear the boy/girl buzz from your junior high daughter or you have an older teen who's had relationships, maybe even some that left her an emotional wreck, this book can rescue you and your daughters from future dating disasters. We've included structured discussion activities in Chapter 10 that you can do as a family. Each activity is designed to help you get the conversation ball rolling. By discussing the issue of dating and its related subjects, you and your family will be able to come up with your own family dating policy. A family dating policy contains the rules (for example, you can date when you're 16), limits (date nights will be Fridays and Saturdays), and expectations (never get in your date's car if he's been drinking) that honor the rights of teens and the concerns of parents.

Whatever policy your family ultimately creates, it should reflect the values and goals that are important to you. Every family is different, and the age(s) and experience(s) of your daughter(s) will influence the rules you establish. The most important thing is that you and your family start talking about dating relationships and figuring out answers to questions like these:

- What does "dating" mean?
- Who is dateable?
- What is the curfew on date night?
- Can I date on a school night?
- Who pays for what?
- Can I "make" someone go out with me?
- What is love?

We hope you use this book as a tool for teaching your daughters how to have better, healthier dating experiences. Of course, when you start discussing dating relationships with your daughters, be prepared for eye-rolling or indignation. Try not to be discouraged. You probably will hear, "This is SOOO stupid!" or "You guys are such dweebs," or "My friends don't do this stupid stuff with their parents." The best reply to this last comment is to say, "I'll be happy to share this book with your friends' parents." Even if your kids tell you they don't care what you think, that isn't necessarily true.

Cute Canine or Killer Cujo?

One evening our daughter's date showed up at the front door wearing a baseball cap that was pulled so low, it practically obscured the top half of his face. He didn't remove his hat when he stepped inside our house, which was a big mistake. His appearance made our usually sedate dog Sadie (a lab/shepherd mix) go berserk. Sadie barked and lunged at the poor boy, sending him reeling backwards out the front door. Before we could catch Sadie, she had chased the boy across the front lawn and all the way back to his car. The whole time the young man was stumbling backwards and shrieking for help. Needless to say, the date didn't last very long. And he never came back to our house again.

– GRATEFUL PET OWNER

Young people do want to hear from their parents, especially when it comes to the important issues in their lives. A survey conducted by the National Campaign to Prevent Teen Pregnancy revealed that 88 percent of teens believed it would be easier for them to avoid sexual activity if they could speak openly and honestly about the issue with their parents. And 45 percent of teens said their parents have more influence on their decisions about sex than their peers.[1]

As a parent, you love your daughter and want the best for her. When it comes to dating, your gut reaction may be to delay or deny your daughter the experience until she's an adult, or out of the house. We've met parents who didn't trust their daughters enough to let them date unless one parent tagged along – and their daughters were in their late teens! That's not healthy. Kids need to be allowed to go out and try dating. Dating allows them to develop their social skills. Dating teaches them how to interact with members of the opposite sex. And most importantly, dating allows young people to discover the qualities they like and don't like in a partner. So, no matter how overwhelmed or under-prepared you feel, don't go to the extremes of locking up your daughters or leaving them alone to fend for themselves. Take advantage of the fact that you still have them under your roof. When they leave for college or move out of your house, it's too late to have the kind of influence you currently have. Now, you can still be their teacher, counselor, and confidante. You can help them deal with the consequences of their behaviors – good and bad – so they can learn what's really important in relationships.

In the following chapters, we offer some answers – perhaps not as many as you're hoping to find. While it would be wonderful to be able to give you a list of hard-and-fast rules that, if followed, would ensure that your daughter's dating relationships would be perfect, such lists don't exist. Rather than offer up an arbitrary number of etched-in-stone commandments, we want to show you how to have conversations about an aspect of teen life that is too often neglected. Some of the answers you seek are not ours to give. Rather, it's up to you and your family to negotiate what's best for your own health and sanity. Hopefully, the tools and skills we share in these pages will serve to remind you that dating was meant to be fun, not feared.

---

[1] National Campaign to Prevent Teen Pregnancy (2003). *With One Voice 2003: America's Adults and Teens Sound Off About Teen Pregnancy*. Washington, DC: Author.

Chapter 1

The History and Biology of Dating

Don't know much about history
Don't know much biology
Don't know much about science books
Don't know much about the French I took
But I do know that I love you
And I know that if you loved me, too
What a wonderful world this would be...

— WONDERFUL WORLD
BY HERMAN'S HERMITS

Back in 1965, the lyrics to *Wonderful World* captured a "truth" that every love-struck American teen understood: I might not remember when Columbus sailed the ocean blue or know how to pronounce "*je ne sais quoi*," but I know what's really important – love. Four decades later, one could set those lyrics to an urban beat and watch heads nod in unison – to the message as well as the sound.

Kids seem to think they know what love is, and many of them believe they've found love in their dating relationships. How else can you explain the daughter who gets positively giddy every time she has a date, but then turns sour when she finds herself single again? Teens can create so much drama around their dating relationships that many parents are left shaking their heads and asking, "Was it really this complicated when I was that age?" Other parents long for some bygone era, believing that it was somehow easier for kids and parents way back in the day. But that may not be true. A brief history lesson and a look at the latest scientific research suggests there have always been challenges, both external and internal.

Cultural Influences

Just as hairstyles and fashion trends evolve (for better or worse) through the ages, so too do the social rituals surrounding male/female romance. Author Beth Bailey describes the evolution of courtship in her book, *From Front Porch to Back Seat*. In the late 19th century, men would "call" on eligible females. And like today's single man looking for love, there were no guarantees against rejection. Bailey writes, "The young man from the neighboring farm who spent the evening sitting on the front porch with the farmer's daughter was paying a call, and so was the 'society' man who could judge his prospects by whether or not the card he presented at the front door found the lady of his choice 'at home.'"[1]

The calling system of yesteryear was a highly structured and formalized ritual. According to Bailey, women had great sway in the process. Mothers would dictate which callers would be received into their homes, a decision influenced by the familial, social, and financial reputations of the gentleman caller. It was the ladies who also decided which day(s) they would accept callers into their homes and which "days they paid or returned calls."[2] This rather rigid calling process took place in family parlors and at community events such as dances, where guest lists were always highly selective. All of the rules and structures associated with courtship in the 19th century helped to ensure that respectable young ladies were introduced to similarly respectable young lads.

By the 1920s, however, the relative privacy of courtship was being replaced by a much more public display of "dating." According to Bailey, "Dating moved courtship into the public world, relocating it from family parlors and community events to restaurants, theaters, and dance halls. At the same time, it removed couples from the implied supervision of the private sphere – from the watchful eyes of family and local community – to the anonymity of the public sphere."[3]

While women dictated the who, what, and when of the old calling system, the new age of "dating" saw a pronounced power shift toward men and money. In fact, the word "date" originated from the language of the streets, notably prostitutes who used the term to describe their scheduled encounters. Throughout the 20th century, dating – both its meaning and its rituals – would be redefined. In the 1930s and 1940s, America's youth practically elevated dating to a competitive sport, a chance to showcase one's popularity. For men to be successful, they had to have the right possessions – clothing, car, cash – whereas women needed to be "seen with popular men in the 'right' places."[4] For young people, dating was a means to establish popularity. Finding a lifelong mate was secondary.

By the 1950s, going steady became the new symbol of popularity for youth. Boys and girls sought affection from one rather than many. According to Bailey, the concept was disconcerting to adults who worried that young people could not possibly learn anything about the opposite sex if they limited their social interactions to one person. Parents and religious leaders frowned on the idea of going steady for other reasons, too. Many believed it made a couple more likely to engage in premarital sex. For young people, however, finding someone to go steady with was a stress reducer. With a steady, they had a guaranteed date to formals, and they didn't have to continually compete against their peers for dates to every social event. For them, security trumped competition.[5]

> "I'm dating a woman now who, evidently, is unaware of it."
>
> – GARY SHANDLING
> COMEDIAN

In the following decades, dating relationships would be turned upside down by changes in American society. There was the sexual revolution and women's liberation in the 1960s and 1970s. There were latchkey kids and deadly sexually transmitted diseases in the 1980s. By the dawn of the new millennium, communication technologies transformed everyday life. Young people from every corner of the globe were suddenly connected in their own virtual communities. Instant messaging and personal cell phones have replaced the family phone as the primary communications tool. Now, parents are denied complete access to who their children are contacting and vice versa. Many of the built-in mechanisms that existed within families and communities to monitor a child's social interactions are gone, and they aren't coming back. Even the lingo of youth culture makes it difficult for today's parents to know exactly what's going on.

Talkin' about love

The language of modern relationships bears little resemblance to anything used in previous generations. And it's constantly changing. Much of young people's lingo is taken from rap lyrics and teen movies, two forms of media that parents rarely tune in to. Even words or phrases that are native to one corner of the globe can become universally adopted thanks to the Internet. If you heard your daughter use the word "baggin'," would you know that she's picking up a guy? Maybe your son refers to a girl as "breezy"; would you know that she was his girlfriend? Or if you heard a group of your daughter's friends talking about "givin' up the gold," would you know they were referring to losing one's virginity? Even if you knew what these slang words meant, by the time you finish reading this book, new words will likely have taken their place, if they haven't already. In modern America, the euphemisms of youth culture change as frequently as teens change their iPod playlists.

So is there anything we can learn from the past to help us understand our children's dating environment? The best lesson may be realizing that there really never was a "golden age" of dating. Wishing for a return to the simple, stress-free good ol' days (that never existed) will leave you ill prepared for what's happening today. Whether it was the young gentleman struggling to understand the etiquette of making a social call in 1905 America or the 13-year-old hottie taking a booty call via text messaging in modern America, dating has never been easy for most kids or enjoyable for their parents. Every generation has been, and will be, influenced by the culture and realities of its time. That won't change, and neither will the stress it causes parents.

Biological Influences

Here's a newsflash: Girls and boys are different. Just as the world intrudes on relationships, so too does biology. Aside from the obvious physical features that distinguish the genders, the mental makeup of girls and boys is anything but identical. In *Brain Sex: The Real Difference Between Men and Women*, authors Anne Moir and David Jessel tell readers, "The sexes are born with brains wired in different ways. They think in different ways, have different strengths, value things in a different way, and use different strategies to approach life. These brain biases are accentuated and refined throughout life, particularly when spurred on by the hormonal surge of adolescence."[6]

While a man's brain is biased toward objects and activities, the female's brain is biased toward people and relationships. These biases influence behavior. As Moir and Jessel note, "The boy more naturally involves himself in experiences that sharpen spatial skills; the girl involves herself more in experiences that strengthen interpersonal skills. Boys want to explore areas, spaces, and things because their brain bias predisposes them to these aspects of the environment. Girls like to talk and listen because that is what their brains are better designed to do."[7]

But what do brain differences have to do with your daughter's dating relationships? Plenty.

In adolescence, the brain is still a work in progress. For example, the prefrontal cortex is the region of the brain that is thought to play an important role in our ability to make connections between actions and consequences. This part of our brain is charged with helping us solve problems, plan, and make judgments. It also plays a role in our inhibitions, or lack thereof. For teens whose hormones are already raging, there's one thought they all seem to share: "If it feels good, do it." And they do. They're impulsive. The emotional, sometimes irrational decisions teens make can be partly or totally attributed to the fact that their brains are still developing. Their brains are like a computer with a file manager that isn't fully loaded. Things misfire and go haywire. Anthropologist Helen Fisher, quoted in Barbara Strauch's book, *The Primal Teen*, says, "The prefrontal cortex develops slowly. They [teens] have strong drives but not the brain power or the experience to go with them."[8] Neuroscientist Dr. Jay Giedd puts it this way: "They have the passion and the strength but no brakes and they may not get good brakes until they are twenty-five."[9]

> "When you are courting a nice girl an hour seems like a second. When you sit on a red-hot cinder a second seems like an hour. That's relativity."
>
> – ALBERT EINSTEIN
> RENOWNED PHYSICIST

As parents, we need to understand that even if our teenage daughters look physically mature, they are not grown up. Most still lack the cognitive development necessary to fully comprehend the consequences of their choices. In other words, even teens still need their parents. That's why child psychiatrist Peter Jensen tells moms and dads that it will sometimes be their responsibility to be the "prefrontal cortex" for their teenagers.[10]

The 'cuddle hormone'

While this isn't a biology book, we do want to mention that it's not just your daughter's brain that influences her behavior. Her hormones are at work as well. One in particular may play a pivotal role in her relationships. Oxytocin, also referred to as the "cuddle" or "prosocial" hormone, is believed to facilitate social bonding, whether that bond is between a mother and her newborn or two starry-eyed lovers. Oxytocin's effect on female behavior may be as potent as testosterone's effect on males. Although it's found in both sexes, oxytocin in females helps to stimulate milk production, uterine contractions, and maternal behavior. But new research also suggests it may have a powerful influence on intimate relationships. Oxytocin is naturally released in males and females in response to a variety of stimuli, including sexual feelings or activities. Neuroscientist Diane Witt describes the power that this bonding hormone can have on a girl's dating life: "You first meet him and he's passable. The second time you go out with him, he's OK. The third time you go out with him, you have sex. And from that point on you can't imagine what life would be like without him."[11]

Children of the Corn

My best friend Shawna's new boyfriend asked her to go to a festival in his hometown. Shawna invited me to tag along with them. I didn't know her boyfriend that well, and I had never met his friends, but it sounded fun, so I agreed to go. We were all having a great time at the festival when Shawna's boyfriend said, "Everybody's going out to the pond. Let's go." Shawna didn't know what the "pond" was, nor did I. Her boyfriend drove us a mile out of town to a pasture with a shallow creek, surrounded by cornfields. It was dark when we arrived, and there were maybe 20 or 30 other kids hanging out. There was at least one keg and Bon Jovi was blaring from a boom box. I told Shawna I didn't want to stay. She didn't either, but her date and his friends shouted at us to follow them. We hung back by the car thinking we would leave soon. As we stood there, we watched and laughed at all the girls who wandered into the field to relieve themselves. Little did we know we'd soon be "children of the corn," too.

We weren't there more than 10 minutes when someone shouted, "Cops are coming!" Suddenly, everyone went running. Shawna and I darted into the cornfield. The stalks were taller than we were, and the ground was uneven. Shawna was running ahead of me and tripped. I fell over her and took out a half-dozen corn stalks on my way down. By the time we reached the end of the row, Shawna had lost her shoes, and my arms were scratched from the corn stalks. We looked around for Shawna's date and his friends, but we didn't see them. We did see the lights of the town in the distance, so we headed that way. Of course, we had to climb over a barbed-wire fence to get out of the field. I got caught on the wire as I climbed over, ripped my jeans, fell forward, and planted my face in the dirt. Shawna lost her footing, too. She fell and rolled down into the ditch. We eventually made it back into town and caught a ride home. Shawna dumped her boyfriend the next day, and we never saw him or his friends again.

– Ditched on a Group Date

The bonding power of oxytocin may explain why some girls who are sexually intimate with their partners turn into emotional zombies or behave as if a death occurred in the family following a romantic breakup. The depth of their attachment, fueled by oxytocin, may produce profound despair, yet another unexpected and unwanted consequence for the sexually active teen.

What Parents Can Do

So, is parental influence powerless against the tides of history and biology? Has our daughters' fate already been sealed inside their genetic makeup and the prevailing cultural trends? We don't think so.

History simply shows us that it's impossible to reclaim the unclaimable. Dating used to involve tremendous thought, supervision, stringent ritual, and community effort. It was also very controlling. Adults dictated who did what, when, and with whom. The child's voice was virtually silent compared to today's standards. And the process itself could be discriminatory, denying potential relationships on the basis of race, religion, or riches. It wasn't perfect then, nor is it realistic now. The current dating environment also leaves much to be desired. Structure has given way to chaos, as young people engage in a seemingly endless string of hookups and breakups. They don't know what they want out of their relationships, nor do they know how to get it if they do know. At the same time, parents are pushed to the sidelines and their voices – by choice or circumstance – are silenced. Surely we can find a happier and healthier medium between the dictatorship of the past and the aimless drift of today.

In our experience, parents who are forthright and willing to talk to their daughters about dating, including the social skills it requires, have less stress and fewer sleepless nights. And their daughters enjoy more rewarding experiences. But when girls are left to figure things out on their own, in the absence of parental guidance, they often find themselves in dysfunctional relationships. To help your daughter overcome and avoid dating pitfalls, you have to talk to one another, ask questions, and listen. In the next chapter, we show you how to have a running conversation in your family that can help your daughters learn how to date wisely.

---

[1] Bailey, Beth L. *From Front Porch to Back Seat: Courtship in Twentieth-Century America*. Baltimore: The Johns Hopkins University Press (1989) p. 15.

[2] Ibid.

[3] Ibid., p. 13.

[4] Ibid., p. 26.

[5] Ibid.

[6] Moir, Anne and Jessel, David. *Brain Sex: The Real Difference Between Men and Women*. New York: Carol Publishing Group (1991) p. 100.

[7] Ibid., pp. 58-59.

[8] Strauch, Barbara. *The Primal Teen: What the New Discoveries About the Teenage Brain Tell Us About Our Kids*. New York: Doubleday (2003) p. 150.

[9] Ibid., p. 33.

[10] Ibid., p. 34.

[11] Diane Witt, quoted in Susan E. Barker, "'Cuddle Hormone' Research Links Oxytocin and Socio-Sexual Behaviors," Oxytocin.org, http://www.oxytocin.org/cuddle-hormone.

Chapter 2

Don't Say 'Ugh' to Dating

"I can handle the crushes my daughter has on every bad-boy actor that turns up on one of her favorite TV dramas. I think it's kind of funny. Of course, it's easier to laugh when you know those guys won't be pulling into the driveway to whisk her away to who knows where. But when she told me she wanted to 'go out' with Chip from chemistry class, I froze. He's not some guy on the silver screen, he's Chip the lab partner. He's real. He may be her dreamboat, but he's my nightmare."

— Nervous Dad

This father definitely sounds as if he's saying "Ugh!" to the idea of his daughter dating. His gloom is not unlike that of many parents caught off guard by daughters who are as eager to enjoy a night out with the boys as they are with their gal pals. Although he has misgivings, this dad obviously is involved in his child's life. He knew the prospective date's name, and how they met. That's a good start. In some homes, girls don't even bother to ask if they can go out; they just do. And some parents don't bother to find out where, or with whom, their teens go. The parent might say, "Be home by midnight," but offer no other boundaries or seek any other details. That's unfortunate. This aspect of teen life shouldn't scare you into silence, nor should you trivialize its value. Dating, like any other family issue, deserves attention and demands a rational, responsible approach.

Having 'The Talk'

"The Talk" is what we call the **first** serious discussion you and your daughter have about love and dating. Of course, there can't be just one. Open and honest communication about your daughter's relationships should be frequent. But in a lot of families, parents try to wing it. They might ask an occasional question, but they don't get too concerned or involved unless they see a problem. This reactive approach contributes to the chaos surrounding many teen relationships. That's why we recommend that parents call time out, sit down with their daughters, and seriously discuss dating. It doesn't matter if your daughter is about to go on her first date or her twenty-first; if you haven't talked about what dating relationships mean, or how they affect the whole family, you need to. The trick, of course, is having a conversation that won't dissolve into a joke or a shouting match.

So, how do you bring up the subject? What do you talk about? Is it better to wait until your daughter comes to you with a concern before you say anything? Should you do all the talking if she's not willing to share? How do you broach the subject with an older teen who may think it's none of your business? These are the questions nervous parents often ask us. The truth is that there is no one perfect way. However, there are things you can do to facilitate better communication. Having a plan to guide your discussion can go a long way toward making the conversation worthwhile, which makes future chats that much easier to have.

Plan ahead and structure your talk.

Schedule a specific time to sit down and chat. Pick a day that doesn't conflict with any other obligations you or your daughter may have. Tell her you've been reading this book and thought it would be a good idea if, as a family, you sat down and talked about dating. If she enjoys going out for dinner, you might suggest having the conversation at her favorite restaurant. Or, if she has a favorite coffee or juice shop, you might go there. Wherever you decide to have your special talk, it should be a place that's comfortable and free of lots of distractions.

Prepare a list of thought-provoking questions.

To keep the conversation focused, try writing down key talking points in the form of questions. (Five questions that we recommend are listed on page 25.) You and your daughter should answer these questions separately **before** you get together to talk. The questions should delve into how prepared your daughter is to date safely and successfully. The questions also should identify everyone's expectations and determine whether or not they are the same. Do your daughter's attitudes about love and ideas about who is dateable jibe with your own? If not, is that good or bad? It's better to give your daughter the list of questions in advance (at least two days) so she has time to think and reflect. You'll probably need that same amount of time to really think through your answers. Let her know that you are answering the questions and that you'll discuss each other's responses when you get together.

Everyone should write down their thoughts and feelings to each question. We've found that writing encourages kids and parents to think more critically about the issue. The concepts become more real. When answers are not written down, you tend to hear lots of "I guess so," or "I don't know." The conversation can easily drift into irrelevant areas, leaving important issues unresolved. Writing is also a popular activity with girls, so motivating your daughter to write down her thoughts shouldn't be a problem. However, if you don't think she will take the questions seriously, tie consequences to her behavior. For example, a negative consequence for blowing them off (maybe she writes down silly one- or two-word answers or leaves questions blank) could be not allowing her to date until she honestly shares her thoughts with you. On the other hand, if she is open and agreeable, you should praise her honesty and maturity.

When you're discussing love and relationships, don't avoid certain topics because you're afraid of what you might hear. It's better to have a conversation and learn what's going on so you can provide support and guidance. Remember, this will be the first of (hopefully) many conversations that will help you create a family dating policy. The answers to these big-picture questions can shape and influence the specific dating rules your family may want or need. You might even discover that your daughter isn't ready to be in a dating relationship. The best way to find out is to ask these five questions:

1. **What does dating mean?**
2. **What is the purpose of dating?**
3. **What is love?**
4. **Who is dateable?**
5. **What expectations do you have about dating?**

Questions Asked and Answered

We don't know how you or your daughter will respond to these questions. What we do know is that you'll probably be in for some surprises. You might be pleased at how similar your daughter's answers are to your own. You might be delighted by the depth and maturity of her responses. Or, her answers may leave you disappointed, even angry. If she says something that shocks, hurts, or baffles you, do your best to remain calm. Swallow, as best you can, your anger. Try not to mock or dismiss her opinions. A more constructive approach is to continue the dialogue by asking her why she feels a particular way. You can calmly insert your own feelings with questions that begin, "Have you ever thought about this?"

The point of asking and answering these questions is to help you and your daughter clarify your values and expectations. At the same time, you want to establish some boundaries. Your daughter may have some wonderful ideas about dating relationships, but she also may have some wacky, way-out-there opinions. As the parent, use this conversation to learn more about your daughter and yourself.

What does dating mean?

At first glance, the answer to this question may seem so obvious that it's not worth asking. Trust us when we say you should. This question partially relates back to the lingo of youth culture. Kids are creating new words or putting a new spin on old words to describe their relationships. For instance, we worked with a group of teenage girls who, instead of saying who they were dating, would say, they were "talkin' to him." It meant the same thing. Or a girl would say, "We're talkin.'" Translation: "We're a couple." As a parent, you need to define what your family's dating language will be, regardless of what terms may be in vogue in the wider culture. In your home, your family should have a shared understanding of what words or phrases mean so everyone knows who is who and what is what. For example, some families use the term "boyfriend" to describe any of their daughters' male friends, but call the boys who date their daughters "gentleman callers." Having a common dating language for your family can keep you up to date on the status of your daughter's relationships, including when a boy goes from being a really good pal to her gentleman caller or boyfriend.

There's more to defining what dating means than assigning labels to your daughter's companions. You also want to know what actions constitute dating. Depending on your daughter's age, dating might mean an occasional supervised outing or a weekly social excursion done solo (as in no parents). When we hear junior high kids describe their relationships as "going out," we have to smile. Most aren't going anywhere on a date. They can't, unless a parent or sibling drives them. Usually their "date" refers to the person they hang out with at school or a school-sponsored event. In high school, older teens describe dating as "going to the movies," "going out to eat," "going to prom," etc. We call these activities "car dating." Most young people can visualize and understand this definition – leaving in someone's car or truck without a parent driving or chaperoning. They also know it's more serious than the "dating" that goes on in junior high. (We take a closer look at car dates and "rules for the road" in Chapter 4.)

As you talk, keep in mind that the traditional form of dating – one guy, one gal, and one car – may not be exactly what your modern daughter has in mind. Online dating services are an increasingly popular device teens use to hook up. Access is easy, and often free. According to the Pew Internet and American Life Project, as many as 21 million children between the ages of 12 and 17 go online.[1] To communicate with each other, most use instant messaging. A 2004 *Washington Post* article reported that there were 36 million screen names in use through AOL's free instant-messaging service. Of those, 25 percent belonged to individuals younger than 17.[2] A Pew study also found that 17 percent of adolescents reported using IM to ask someone out. And 13 percent had broken up with someone via instant messaging.[3] Have you given any thought to the possibility your daughter may be cyberdating? In Chapter 7, we look at why online relationships appeal to teens, and why they can be a potential pitfall.

As you discuss what dating means in your family, there are two other issues worth keeping in mind: group dating and solo dating. Group dating remains popular with teens and many parents. For young or inexperienced daters, group dates provide a greater sense of ease and far less pressure. For one thing, no one has to worry about trying to sustain a conversation with a single individual for hours. A trendy form of group dating is "mall dating," where groups of teens gather at a local shopping center to socialize, see a movie, or split some fries at the food court. Parents like the idea of group dates because they believe there's safety in numbers. Do you agree? If so, will you have one set of rules when your daughter is on a group date and a different set of expectations when she pairs off? Pairing off raises still more questions. Is it ever okay for your daughter to be in an exclusive dating relationship? Does your daughter feel if she goes out with a boy once, he automatically becomes her boyfriend? Or, does she look at dating as her chance to play the field and get to know lots of different people? How do you hope she defines dating, and what do you want dating to mean in your family?

As you see, the answer to "what does dating mean" is not always apparent. Many misunderstandings have resulted from the comment, "We're dating," causing heartbreak for teens and headaches for parents. On the bright side, when your family decides on a mutually acceptable definition, then you can start negotiating rules around dating. Chapters 3 through 8 look at how to create dating rules that reflect your daughter's abilities and your family's needs.

What is the purpose of dating?

Here are some of the responses we've heard from teens:

- To make friends
- To be popular

- To "get laid"
- To get out of the house
- To annoy my parents
- To show how much you love someone
- To find a life mate
- Don't know

Answers like these can make anyone leery about letting their teen date. But let's remind ourselves, and our daughters, what the real purpose of teen dating should be: to get to know yourself, make friends, and have fun.

Here's an analogy we like to share with parents to help them see the value of teen dating. You might want to share this with your daughters, too. A high school dating relationship is similar to a Big Wheel or tricycle that Santa put under the tree when your teen was just a toddler. The first time your daughter sat down and pedaled away, she was, in a rudimentary sense, learning how to drive. Of course, you didn't expect her to be behind the wheel of a car in a year or two. Nonetheless, she was learning how to operate a machine. You probably taught her some very basic skills, such as how to avoid mowing down a sibling or neighbor when she tore down the driveway or sidewalk. You were giving her the freedom to explore, albeit under close supervision. Now, dating serves as the training vehicle for your daughter's first foray into the world of relationships. If she is to become socially comfortable and grow up to have healthy adult relationships, she

> The real purpose of teen dating should be to get to know yourself, make friends, and have fun.

has to be allowed to go out on her own at some time. Better for her to learn when she still has you available to provide boundaries, set expectations, and teach values. Dating, just like the Big Wheel, is a fun learning tool. Only now the lessons your daughter learns are about people.

When talking about the purpose of dating, it's a good idea to remind your daughter what her main priorities in life currently are. They don't involve dating, nor having the fullest social calendar. Her main focus – and we hope you agree – should be:

- To be a good student
- To be a good family member
- To be a good person, spiritually and civically

What does being a good student mean? She studies. She completes homework on time. She doesn't skip out on school or activities. She maintains acceptable grades. She follows the rules, and doesn't cheat, bully, or in any way disrupt the learning environment at school.

What does being a good family member mean? She shows respect to her parents and siblings. She honors family obligations, whether it's baby-sitting her younger brother or helping Grandma clean out her garage. She follows family rules on everything from curfews and the use of the car to money matters, including limits on credit card and cash spending.

What does being a good person mean? She works at becoming more other-centered than self-centered. She volunteers in the community or neighborhood. She develops her faith and character.

When she takes personal responsibility for these areas of her life, your daughter is showing the maturity that's needed in dating relationships. But when or if she fails to fulfill her primary obligations, then a dating timeout may be necessary to get her to refocus. Dating should be a privilege that's earned, not a right that's guaranteed.

What is love?

The overwhelming majority of high school romances are fleeting, no matter how many "Nick and Molly FOR-EVER" doodles adorn a notebook. While it may be true that most people aspire to get married some day, teens shouldn't be burdened – by themselves or others – with the expectation that they're auditioning to be someone's future life mate. Most teens aren't ready for that level of love and commitment. First of all, most don't even know what true love is. All kids think love is a feeling. And they tend to see love in Hollywood's most romanticized and idealized image.

Your daughter may ask you if she can be in love. Yes, she can. But what does she mean by that? We've heard teens describe love as "when you want to be around someone." Your daughter may feel all kinds of incredible things toward a boyfriend, but that doesn't mean she should act on her feelings. Kids use "feelings of love" to justify a lot of selfish, silly, and destructive behaviors: ignoring friends, blowing off homework, forgetting family obligations, wasting money, and having sex. When you talk to your daughter about love, help her to understand that there are different kinds of love. Here are four types of love, adapted from authors C.S. Lewis and Mary Beth Bonacci, that we describe for teens to help them realize that true love is much more than a feeling:

Pizza (a.k.a. Friendship) Love – This term is a unique way to quantify love, and one that your daughter should easily understand. There are a lot of teens (and adults) who say they "love" pizza. But how many of them would sacrifice their personal well-being or their life for a slice? Having a deep affection for pizza is one thing, dying for it is quite another. On the love scale, this type of love is much more superficial than unconditional or marriage love. If your teenage daughter says, "But we're in love," ask her if she's prepared to sacrifice her own future for the relationship. Better yet, ask her if the object of her affections is willing to sacrifice his for her. Most teen dating relationships never evolve past the pizza level of "love."

> "Infatuation is when you think he's as sexy as Robert Redford, as smart as Henry Kissinger, as noble as Ralph Nader, as funny as Woody Allen, and as athletic as Jimmy Conners. Love is when you realize that he's as sexy as Woody Allen, as smart as Jimmy Connors, as funny as Ralph Nader, as athletic as Henry Kissinger, and nothing like Robert Redford – but you'll take him anyway."
>
> – Judith Viorst
> American Poet

Infatuation – Many a teen romance has started here. Pure physical attraction or an unexplainable passion leads young hearts to lose perspective, as well as their inhibitions. The trouble with teen relationships built solely on attraction is that they have nothing beyond the physical. They probably don't have a friendship or many shared interests. In fact, these relationships usually collapse when one partner eyes a new hottie with physical endowments he or she finds more appealing. Or a more crushing (and common) scenario is when someone in the relationship is just there for the sex. Once that conquest is made, the relationship ends. When you talk to your daughter about infatuation or sexual desire, you may want to review the discussion we had in the previous chapter about oxytocin. There can be a lot of pressure, even manipulation, for a relationship to become sexual. We've written about the dangers of sexual con artists and dating violence in *Unmasking Sexual Con Games* (see our Recommended Reading on page 209). If your daughter was physically or sexually hurt in a past relationship, this book offers strategies that can protect her from being used or abused again.

Unconditional Love – This love is as deep as infatuation love is shallow. This is the kind of affection shown in healthy families. This love expresses itself through words and behaviors that communicate respect, care, and concern for others. Mother Teresa and Martin Luther King Jr. demonstrated this love throughout their lives. They willingly made great personal sacrifices for the benefit of others. Rare is the 13-, 15-, or 18-year-old who has cultivated this kind of love in their dating relationships. And even if they did, has their partner?

Marriage Love – The deepest expression of love in relationships is marriage love. For marriage love to exist, elements of friendship, physical attraction or chemistry, and unconditional love have to be present. It takes all three, and it must be felt equally by both individuals. One can't build a good life or relationship on sexual love alone. Nor can a relationship sustain itself if only one of the partners is committed to its success.

We should be teaching our children to love well in the purest sense of the word. That means they see others not as objects, but as people. Just as you want the boys in your daughter's life to see her as a special individual, you want your daughter to see young men as individuals who also come from families. They have fathers, mothers, brothers, or sisters who love them, and they don't want the person they care about used or abused either.

If your daughter starts to hate or be cruel to a boy after a breakup, then that relationship was probably doomed from the beginning. Why would she be mean to someone if she considered him a friend? Her behavior is easier to understand when you realize that the best relationships evolve out of friendship. When teen couples separate and then hate, they probably had a faux friendship or their bond was based on superficial things, such as sex appeal or social status. The quality of your daughter's dating experiences will depend a lot on whether or not mutual respect and friendship exist in the relationship.

Who is dateable?

Here are some of the responses we've heard from junior and senior high students:

- Whoever my parents let me
- Older guys who have a car, and a job would be good
- Any hot-looking chick
- Cheerleaders
- Someone who's funny and smart
- Sensitive guys who are outgoing
- Nonsmokers and nondrinkers
- Girls who are nice, not stuck-up
- Jocks are good
- Nobody shorter than me

Do any of these comments remind you of how you and your friends judged others' "dateability"? For teens, the criteria for dateability can be as simple as they are shallow. If your daughter defines dateability in purely superficial terms – the guy wears designer labels, has money to burn, drives a tricked-out set of wheels, or looks hot – how will you respond? We've heard more than a few teens say that they sometimes feel pressure to date people who have a certain look or certain level of popularity. Some even measure their self-worth by who's on their arm. Pressure from peers plus ego-driven desires can have a powerful influence on

Romantic Hollywood

Hollywood is very good at projecting a picture of romance that leaves audiences weak-kneed and wistful:

- "Kiss me. Kiss me as if it were the last time."
  – Ingrid Bergman's Ilsa in *Casablanca*
- "I would rather have had one breath of her hair, one kiss from her mouth, one touch of her hand, than eternity without it."
  – Nicholas Cage's Seth in *City of Angels*
- "You had me at 'hello'."
  – Renée Zellweger's Dorothy in *Jerry Maguire*

The idealized, romanticized depictions of love and relationships seen on screen are desired by many but attained by few. These romantic fairy tales can be so appealing and seem so attainable that young people, even some adults, expect their relationships to be as idyllic. But no one can live up to the make-believe. Expecting that someone will only creates a disappointing ending.

who your daughter thinks is dateable. A little superficiality is understandable. For many teens, hooking up with a high-status peer is much more appealing than getting stuck with someone who is "nice" but socially lost. On the other hand, what if your daughter says dateability depends on the heart and what's inside a person – personality, brains, trustworthiness, or sincerity? Sounds better than artificial symbols of attractiveness, right? Well, values like trustworthiness and sincerity are abstract. Does your daughter know what it means to be sincere or trustworthy, and can she identify those traits in potential dates?

The dateability question is a great opportunity to put abstract values into concrete terms that make sense to your daughter. For example, when we discuss trustworthiness with girls, we explain how trustworthy individuals possess and repeatedly demonstrate four special characteristics: integrity (the courage to resist temptation); honesty (the ability to be sincere and be truthful); reliability (the willingness to honor commitments); and loyalty (the strength to stand with someone in need). Do girls want boyfriends who are loyal? Yes. Do girls want boyfriends who are honest? Yes. Do girls want boyfriends who make wise decisions? Yes. Do girls want boyfriends they can depend on? Yes. Do girls sometimes still choose relationships with more style than substance? Yes. Will your daughter? Probably; after all, she is still a teenager. One of the reasons you should talk about dateability is to help broaden your daughter's perspective. You want to help her think more critically about values that she may have never thought much about. A guy's material possessions can be important, but do you want your daughter to value things more than people? Saying a guy is dateable because he's sweet sounds sensible. But is a guy "sweet" because he buys his girl gifts every time he acts like a jerk, or is he sweet because he is thoughtful, respectful, and considerate? There's a difference. One is manipulative, the other genuine.

As you talk about dateability, ask your daughter to think about her friendships and what makes them so special to her. We do this exercise with teens, and it's a real eye-opener for many of them. The characteristics of a real friend are great traits to have in a dating partner. Real friendship is:

Reciprocal – Both friends like one another and consider the other a friend.

Sharing – Friends share common interests and experiences together, and are there for each other during both good and bad times.

Inclusive – Both have other friends; new friends are always welcome. The friendship is not exclusive.

Based on trust – Friends rely on each other, stand up for each other, and keep their word.

Honest – Friends tell the truth, even when it may be hard to do so.

Respectful – Friends treat others with dignity; they don't put down, control, bully, or manipulate others.

Caring – A friend has the other person's best interests in mind.

The Name Game

My dad would sometimes play mind games with the boys that I and my three sisters dated. If Dad didn't like one of our dates or boyfriends, he would intentionally and repeatedly call the guy by the wrong name. I remember a boy named Daryl that I dated. It didn't take me long to figure out my dad didn't approve of him. Every time Daryl came to the house to pick me up, Dad greeted him at the door with a hardy handshake and a friendly, "Nice to see you again, Darren." Daryl would politely correct him, but to no avail. By the time we were walking out the door, usually only a few minutes later, Dad would shout out, "Bye Darren." My sisters and I usually got a good laugh out of it, but the boys were completely baffled.

– DAUGHTER OF A CUNNING AND COMIC FATHER

Before your family finishes its discussion about what makes someone a good date, ask your daughter if she's dateable. Self-reflection can be a good reality check. Sometimes, the standards expected from others are more than we can meet ourselves. Dating relationships require two persons' participation, but no matter how wonderful the guy may be, it won't mean a thing if your daughter lacks the social skills, temperament, or judgment to handle the relationship. (In Chapter 3, we look at how you can measure your daughter's dating readiness by considering much more than her chronological age.)

What expectations do you have about dating?

This question has left many teens, and nearly as many parents, silent. For some young people, it's hard to think about the future when their motivations have everything to do with the present. When teens see their friends pairing up, they think they have to do the same just to fit in. To not be dating is to run the risk of being left out or labeled a "loser." The same message is reinforced in teen magazines with headlines that scream, "10 ways to get a guy to like you" or "Five hairstyles to make guys take notice." Girls are told that they have to have a boyfriend, and too many buy into the idea that their self-worth is derived from having one. Some become so desperate, they try to force relationships. But once they corner a "date," they're left wondering, "What now?"

"What now" goes right to the heart of dating expectations and brings the conversation full circle.

As you talk about expectations, you should gain insight into some of the motivations your daughter has for wanting to date. Whatever motivates your daughter to be in a dating relationship will influence the kind of expectations she has. For example, you may discover that her motives are driven more by peer pressure than personal desire. Therefore, one of her expectations may be that dating will allow her to hang with the "in crowd." If she's boy crazed, she may use dating to elevate her appeal with guys she's interested in, but not involved with. Or, maybe she has a real adventurous spirit. Her only expectation might be to meet new people and have fun experiences.

Any discussion about expectations probably will require explanation. We've seen enough blank expressions to know that most teens haven't given this much, if any, deliberate thought. First of all, teens hear the word "expectations" and get intimidated. Many wonder why they need to bother with, or worry about, the long view. Remember, their brains are telling them to live in the moment and if it feels good, do it. Others assume expectations mean making grand, profound pronouncements about how dating will be a life-altering experience. (That is a reality-check moment in which teens should be gently reminded that some, maybe a lot, of dates will be more forgettable than phenomenal.) Your daughter may struggle to identify her expectations, or she might have expectations that are simply unrealistic. Whichever scenario you face with your teen, we suggest keeping expectations focused on the simple, fundamental elements of dating:

- How do you want to feel after a date?
- How do you want to be treated on a date?
- How should you treat others on a date?
- What activities/places make a good date?

These are the kinds of expectations that will do more good for your daughter than those dealing with how to snare a spouse. When teen romances end, and most do eventually, the girls who are less resilient are those who created a fantasy future with their boyfriends. They thought they had the "perfect" relationship, just like the ones they read about in teen magazines or see on the silver screen. Their expectations exceeded reason. They end up blaming themselves or their boyfriends for why the relationship failed. The real problem wasn't the behavior of any one individual as much as it was the burden of unreasonable expectations placed on the relationship. You can help your daughter keep her expectations from spiraling out of control by emphasizing the present, not the future. Keep the focus on how to be, and have, a good date. Everything else after that will take care of itself.

More Talking Tidbits

Having "The Talk" should occur regardless of your family's situation. In two-parent households, both parents need to be present and participate in the conversation. If you're divorced or separated from your spouse, share this book with him or her. Hopefully, both of you can agree that a family dating policy is important and that both of you need to be consistent in the rules and boundaries you set for your daughter. If that's not possible, at least let your kids know what you believe and what your expectations are for them. Single parents shouldn't be intimidated by any of the activities included in this book either. You can do this, too! If you're unsure about answering any of these questions, feel free to bounce ideas off someone whose opinion you value, whether it's a relative, friend, neighbor, co-worker, or spiritual advisor. Whatever your particular situation happens to be, don't forget that your role is still to be the parent. If you don't talk to your daughter, who will? What will she hear? What will she do?

Once you have a handle on what's going on in your daughter's life and how she feels about dating relationships, you can start to negotiate some rules that will be good for her and comfortable for you. We can't possibly think of or write about every conceivable situation in which you would want a family rule. If we did, this book would never end. That's why we've chosen to look at the areas of teen dating that seem to cause families the most conflict. They also happen to be the areas where few, if any, boundaries are established until after problems arise: Age (How old do you want your daughter to be before she starts dating and what age should her dates be?); Car Dates (If she's old enough to handle a car, is she old enough to handle her date?); Appropriate Dress (When skin is in, is a bare midriff, backless dress, or plunging neckline being fashionable or foolish?); Gift Giving (Are gifts of underwear going over the top?); Internet (Are virtual relationships a safer, better alternative for your daughter?); and The Breakup (Is breaking up really hard to do?).

 Use humor and honesty to kick start a family discussion on love and relationships. The ice-breaker activities on pages 175 and 177 are a great way to begin.

1 Pew Internet and American Life Project. (2005). Protecting Teens Online [Online]. Available: http://www.pewinternet.org/pdfs/ PIP_Filters_Report.pdf.

2 Edwards, E. "Buddy Lists and Mixed Messages," *The Washington Post Online*, http://www.washingtonpost.com/wp-dyn/articles/ A64312-2004May3.html.

3 Pew Internet and American Life Project. (2001). Teenage Life Online [Online]. Available: http://www.pewinternet.org/pdfs/PIP_Teens_ Report.pdf.

Chapter 3

Age Is More
Than a Number

*"My girlfriend used to ask her father, 'How can I
find the right man for me?' and he would answer,
'Don't worry about finding the right man – con-
centrate on becoming the right woman.'"*

— ANONYMOUS

When it comes to family dating rules, the most heated
discussions can erupt around the question of when. When
is your daughter old enough to start dating? Junior high?
High school? College? There are many advice books and online "dating experts" who answer this question with vague
statements, such as "when you think your teen is ready,"
or arbitrarily pick an age, like 16, because of its historical
significance or their own personal experience. But does
being 16 automatically make someone more ready to date
than someone who is 14? Sixteen can be quite reasonable
for some girls, but it can be way too early for others. Why
does one family allow their 13-year-old to date while another family says no dating until 17? Did they read different

advice columns? Did the parents of the 13-year-old have a feeling their daughter could handle herself, while the other parents felt 17 made more sense? As you look at your own daughter, how will you judge her dating readiness?

Junior High-Jinks

There are two boy-related questions that every junior high girl seems desperate to answer:

- How can I make him like me?
- How can I make him be my boyfriend if he just wants to be friends?

Our answer to the first question can be crushing to those with crushes: "You can't, so get over it." Our answer to the second question doesn't do much to lift a fluttering heart either: "You can't make him do anything, so stop trying." But why are these questions so common and our responses so certain?

Junior high is a tricky time for adolescent girls. Their giddiness and excitement about dating relationships is rarely shared by their male peers. Most boys that age just want to hang with their buddies and toss a ball around. In fact, more than a few junior high guys complain that a girl's desire to date or have a boyfriend gives them all kinds of grief. There are the embarrassing love notes wedged into the corners of a locker. There are the nightly barrages of "like, don't you like me" instant messages. There are incessant phone calls and hang-ups. There are even confrontations in the cafeteria. And these aggressive acts are not instigated solely by the smitten girl who's on the prowl for her special guy. Inevitably their friends get dragged into the drama. All of a

I Need a Girlfriend by Friday

In seventh grade, my son (Cameron) was best friends with Stevie. Stevie was a nice kid, but he was definitely maturing faster than my son and the other boys. Stevie had the hots for a girl from their class and invited her to the movies on a Friday night. The girl's parents apparently said that was fine, provided it wasn't going to be just the two of them. They told her other kids had to go along. I guess her parents thought that would be safer. Anyway, the girl told Stevie she could go but only if another "couple" joined them. Stevie then told my son, on Tuesday morning, that he had to ask someone to the movies before Friday. Otherwise, he'd ruin Stevie's chances with this girl, and if that happened, Stevie wouldn't talk to him again.

Cameron came home from school that day in a panic. In a very serious tone, he said, "I have to have a girlfriend by Friday." He explained the situation, as convoluted as it was. Thinking I was being rational and helpful, I told Cameron that he could go to the movie, but he didn't have to have a girlfriend. I suggested that Stevie's girl ask one of her friends to tag along and that he go as Stevie's friend. The look that came over Cameron's face told me it was the stupidest idea he'd ever heard. "Mom," he said, "if I show up, the other girl will assume I'm her date. And if I ask a girl to go, she'll think she's my GF and I'll get stuck with her. Don't you know anything about girls in junior high?"

– HAPPILY CLUELESS MOM

sudden you have a group of girls chasing around a group of guys, trying to force declarations of love and create "perfect" couples. What's worse is that the behaviors keep repeating themselves. The girls look desperate, and the guys get annoyed. It's as if some girls don't care what a guy says today because they think he will have a change of heart tomorrow. But he won't. That's why we tell girls straight up to accept reality. They need to hear the truth from someone because they aren't hearing it from their friends. Healthy dating relationships start with friendship, not with force or duress.

Personal Boundaries and Dating Readiness

The stalking or hounding behaviors that go on in junior high, and high school, relate back to our discussion in Chapter 2 about dateability. If your daughter really digs someone, but he's not that into her, can she accept the fact that he's not dateable right now or will she play games until he gives in or gives up? Any 20- or 30-something who's single and dating will tell you that calendar age means nothing when it comes to emotional maturity. The adult dating scene is littered with failed relationships that were undone by poor communication, immature behaviors, unreasonable expectations, and one-sided control. These same troubles cloud the teen dating scene. The critical difference is that young people possess even less experience and fewer interpersonal skills that can help them avoid or overcome these problems. Age alone is not a reliable predictor of dating success. But what is? Your daughter's actions and attitudes will tell you far more than the number of candles atop her birthday cake about her relationship readiness.

As a general rule, we think dating relationships are unwise and unnecessary for youth who are still in junior high. Now you might think, given that we just said age should not be the only criteria for determining dating readiness, that we're contradicting ourselves. How can we suggest such a blanket rule for an entire group based on nothing more than age? Our experience, and research, suggests that young teens simply can't handle dating relationships for reasons that have as much to do with their emotional intelligence and social abilities as their age. Plus, there are alternatives to dating relationships (especially exclusive ones) that are just as rewarding but offer far fewer risks. If you have a daughter in junior high who is dating or is begging to have a boyfriend, consider the potential pitfalls:

The sexual temptations

Pre-teens and young teens (14, 15, and 16) already are dealing with all sorts of external pressures. We know, for example, that bullying reaches its nastiest peak in junior high. There's a lot of stress on kids to fit in and be socially accepted by their peers. There's academic pressure. Each passing year brings more challenging coursework and testing. Parents can add to the pressure by demanding excellence in the classroom or on the athletic field. Many young people get involved in so many extracurricular activities, they feel stress just trying to meet all of their obligations. Kids are getting pulled in many directions and have lots of distractions. Should the demands of maintaining a dating relationship be part of the mix, too? All relationships have moments of stress, and young romance can create situations few teens are prepared to handle. Here is a story one parent shared with us:

Elle was a 14-year-old dynamo with a big crush on her eighth-grade classmate, Brady. Elle wasn't shy about much, including expressing her feelings. She flirted with Brady at school, wrote him notes, and sent e-cards to his Hotmail account. Her messages were full of typical teen drama about hating school and having clueless parents, but she also included lines about how much she liked the way Brady dressed and how funny she thought he was. It only took a couple weeks of flirting before Elle had Brady as her boyfriend. Brady's parents didn't give much thought to the relationship until the day Brady's stepmom found one of Elle's hand-written notes lying on his bed. What she read stunned her. Elle wrote in great detail about how much she enjoyed having sex with Brady. When Brady's stepmom got over her initial shock, she decided to take the note to Elle's mom before confronting her son. Elle's mother was equally hurt by her daughter's revelation. Surprisingly, the moms didn't blame the other's child for what happened. Instead, they agreed that the relationship had to immediately change, and that it was important for their children to be tested for sexually transmitted diseases. They also agreed to put major restrictions on the relationship. The moms didn't forbid the two from ever seeing each other again; they felt that was too unrealistic. They didn't want to create a Romeo and Juliet situation, and besides, the kids attended the same school. But they did limit where and when the two could socialize. And any interactions the two had outside of school had to be chaperoned.

> "True love comes quietly, without banners or flashing lights. If you hear bells, get your ears checked."
>
> – ERICH SEGAL
> AMERICAN AUTHOR

Elle was angry at her mom and Brady. She couldn't believe he would be so careless as to leave her note lying around. But Brady wasn't being careless; he was crying out for help. He intentionally left the note on his bed, hoping his stepmom would see it when she cleaned his room. Brady told his parents that he didn't want to be having sex, but he felt trapped. He was too embarrassed to tell his girlfriend he didn't want to be that intimate, but he didn't know how to stop it from happening again. That's why he left the note out. He was embarrassed and too ashamed to talk directly with his parents. His way of reaching out was to leave clues for them to find.

You may think we made this story up, or flipped the facts to make the girl look like the sexual predator instead of the usual guy. We didn't. But imagine how many young girls are out there who, like Brady, don't know how to say no to their partners. How many feel pressured to put out, then, once they've "givin' up the gold," think there's no point in ever saying "No" again? There is some research that suggests young teens in exclusive dating relationships are more likely to engage in sexual activity. That's not true for every relationship, but the temptation and curiosity is always there.

The poor communication

As young teens, girls and boys have strikingly different communication preferences and abilities. Girls make friends by talking. Boys make friends by doing. Girls enjoy being on the phone or instant messaging on the computer for hours at a time. That's something most of their male peers have little desire to do, at least for that long. And when girls direct all of that phone or online time toward boys, most of the parents of those young men don't appreciate it. All the notes that fly back and forth at school and the instant messages that pop up on the computer can make girls look desperate. They may think they're being assertive, but they're actually behaving aggressively. And for what? A relationship that, at best, will probably only last a few weeks but could damage their reputations for years.

Perhaps the biggest communication problem girls have at this age results from their inability to recognize when they're getting way too personal. A young girl sometimes will share her deepest thoughts and reveal intimate feelings to a boy long before she knows if he can be trusted with such secrets. If he shares what she says with his friends or others at school, the girl will be embarrassed and humiliated. By violating her own personal boundaries, she opens herself up to jokes and ridicule. In junior high, this is an all-too-real scenario.

The inappropriate boundaries

The pitfalls of sexual temptation and poor communication relate to the issue of boundaries. There is a certain physical and emotional distance that teens should keep between themselves and others. These are the boundaries or limits everyone should have in their relationships. Every child needs to know how to establish appropriate physical, emotional, and sexual boundaries, as well as learn how to respect others' personal space. The trouble with most of the dating relationships we see in junior high, and even high school, is that boundaries are always bending or breaking. Some of the most common boundary violations involve:

- Asking very personal questions
- Gossiping about others
- Touching others without their permission
- Revealing private information about someone
- Using offensive, vulgar, or sexually explicit language

- Invading others' private space
- Forcing someone into doing something sexual

As a parent, you can help your daughter set appropriate limits in her relationships. Here are several tips you can share with her on how to establish and maintain good boundaries:

- Avoid people who are selfish, disrespectful, manipulative, or abusive. Such people will likely disrespect you and your boundaries.

- Spend time with people who do well in school and at home, who are liked and respected by many people. They are more likely to have good boundaries themselves and will be more likely to respect your boundaries, too.

- Learn to say "No" when you're being pressured to do something wrong. Anyone who pressures or invites you to do something wrong doesn't respect you or your boundaries.

- Trust your sense of safety or danger. These are good indicators of right and wrong. If someone or something seems dangerous or threatening, stay away!

- Learn how to think through and solve problems before reacting. Problem-solving and critical thinking skills can help you maintain your boundaries and respect others.

- Think about times when your personal boundaries were violated. Who was involved? What was the situation? Think of a better way to handle boundary violations in the future.

- Speak up when someone or something bothers you. Talk to us or other adults you trust.

- When you go out, set limits on where you will go, what you will do, and how long you will be there. Having and sticking to a plan helps you keep and respect boundaries.

- Find ways to tell (or show) others what your personal boundaries are.

Sexual temptations, poor communication, and broken boundaries do not magically disappear after junior high. They present major pitfalls for older teens, too. But what value is there in exposing your daughter to these risks when she's still in junior high, especially when she has other choices? As we mentioned earlier, group dating is popular among teens, and we think it's a much better choice in junior high. Group dates can

> Any activity that allows your daughter to interact naturally with boys without the burden or expectation of being boyfriend and girlfriend is ideal.

ease your teen into dating and offer a more relaxed environment than if she pairs off with someone right away. Group dates also allow your young teen to further develop her personal identity and values. A strong sense of self can reduce the chances of her becoming entangled in unhealthy, manipulative relationships. Even better is the fact that you can help organize and supervise these social outings. Few, if any, junior high kids can drive. They're dependent on Mom and Dad for much of their comings and goings. As a result, you can manage and limit group dates in terms of where, when, and how long. One popular group dating activity that might appeal to your daughter is hosting a movie night or game night at your home. Another group date option could involve volunteer work in the community. Any activity that allows your daughter to interact naturally with boys without the burden or expectation of being boyfriend and girlfriend is ideal. For some girls, discovering that they can just be friends with a boy is a valuable lesson.

Teens and Dating Skills

In junior high, poor judgment, inexperience, and limited social skills make dating relationships unwise. But simply graduating to high school doesn't mean your daughter is any more prepared to start dating. From talking with parents around the country, we've learned that most girls and boys are allowed to go on their first "real" date when they're 16. But the decision to let kids date at 16 seems to be influenced as much, if not more, by the fact that they possess a driver's license and a car, rather than by any personal characteristics they have. Too bad we don't make our kids pass a relationship readiness exam before shuffling them off into the dating scene. If young people took as much time prepping themselves for dating as they do for driving, how many relationship mishaps and meltdowns might be avoided?

As we've been saying, age should not be the primary reason for deciding when dating is okay. Your daughter's social abilities should be. Social skills are the sets of behaviors that give your daughter the ability to interact with others in ways that are socially acceptable and personally beneficial, mutually beneficial, or beneficial to others. By teaching her social skills, you are helping her learn new ways of thinking, new ways of feeling good, and new ways of behaving. The more social skills your daughter has and can use, the better able she will be to handle dating relationships and situations. There are many different social skills, too many to discuss here. However, when it comes to knowing if your daughter is socially and emotionally ready to date, consider how well or how often she demonstrates these important dating skills:

Makes new friends

Every healthy dating relationship starts with friendship. How does your daughter do at being a good friend? For friendship to develop, your daughter has to respect the rights of others. She has to listen to people without putting them down and show interest in what others say and do. Does she? Or, is your daughter more interested in convincing others that her opinions and interests are right or more important? Does she seek out friends who give her stature, but not friendship? One way to measure your daughter's ability to make and have good friendships is to look at the people she surrounds herself with. If she associates with peers who are honest, caring, respectful, and giving, that's a real positive sign that she's developing good judgment and morals. It's quite likely her dating partners will also share those qualities.

Resists negative peer pressure

Would your daughter rather fit in than stand out? Every child has to deal with peer pressure, whether that influence is good or bad. However, it's the negative peer pressure that causes kids trouble. Have you ever heard your daughter agree to a weird idea, bad plan, or stupid suggestion made by her friends? Has she ever stood by and watched someone be bullied at school or in the neighborhood and not done anything? When you tell her she can't go somewhere or do something, does she react with disbelief and whine, "But I'll be the only one who…." or "Everyone will think I'm a…"? If your daughter runs with the crowd in spite of the consequences or her conscience, odds are it will be very difficult for her to say "No" to a date's sexual advances or spurn any other harmful offers.

This is a difficult skill, even for adults. That's why it's important for you to help your daughter learn coping strategies. Here are ways you can teach the skill of resisting negative peer pressure:

- **Teach your daughter to decide for herself whether something is right or wrong, helpful or harmful.** Discuss dating situations that your daughter may find herself in; then explore what might happen if she responds a certain way. Let her think about the consequences of her actions. If she has an uneasy feeling, something is probably wrong.

- **Sometimes, your daughter may just need help getting out of a bad situation. Provide her with some responses she can use to resist the pressure.** Encourage her to avoid giving an immediate "Yes" or "No" answer if a date wants to do something questionable. She can buy time to make a good decision by saying, "Maybe later." Let her use you as an excuse: "I will be grounded forever if I try that" or

"My parents will never let me see you again if we do this."

- **Practice situations with your daughter, and have her try various responses that she is comfortable saying.** Go on a practice date with your daughter. Act out different situations she might encounter. Use role-plays to give her a plan she can fall back on if she ever feels pressured. Build her confidence and her ability to say "No."

You can't make peer pressure go away, but teaching your daughter how to deal with it might be the difference between her making a decision she regrets and one she respects.

Maintains healthy relationships

Teens are notorious for being impulsive. Has your daughter ever jumped into a poorly considered friendship or relationship? Some girls have a tendency to totally invest themselves in relationships at the expense of other important people and activities in their lives, including friends, family, school, and work. Those types of relationships have no balance and are disrespectful. Relationships and friendships need perspective and equality. How much balance and respect do you see in your daughter's interactions with family, friends, and others? You can help your daughter examine her relationships to determine which ones are healthy and which ones may need to change or end. Together, consider the following:

- Relationships are not healthy if one person uses the other. Who is giving and who is taking in your relationships?

- Relationships are just one portion of life. Putting too much emphasis on a particular relationship takes away from all the other aspects in your life. Has this ever happened to you? When?

- Relationships are always changing; some will change for the better, some for the worse. What are some ways your relationships have changed?

- Healthy relationships should make you feel safe and comfortable. If you do not feel this way, why not?

- Look at your past relationships, both good and bad, and then describe what each relationship is like now. If it has changed, what happened to change it?

- Identify things that you have done or changed just to please another person. Did the other person also change?

Teaching your daughter how to think more critically about her relationships will help her avoid a harmful friendship and feeling trapped. Self-reflection will also point out the behaviors and actions she needs to improve in order to be a better friend to others.

Teens with healthy boundaries . . .

- Are secure about themselves.
- Have a clear sense of their own views, values, and priorities.
- Are confident.
- Can protect themselves without shutting off from others.
- Know how to stand up for themselves at appropriate times and in appropriate ways.
- Are able to enter into relationships without losing their own identity.

Handles rejection appropriately

As children grow, they experience moments of acceptance (a warm embrace from a parent) and rejection (a cold shoulder from a classmate). Unfortunately, some young people respond to rejection in extreme ways. Some project their disappointment outward and reject the rejecters. Not being chosen for the team makes them hate the sport. Not being invited to the party makes them bitter toward those who were. Others turn their disappointment inward. They see rejection as confirmation of a perceived flaw – too dumb, too weird, too fat, too ugly, etc. Sadly, the only lesson some seem to learn from rejection is to hate – themselves or others.

When it comes to dating, rejection is going to happen. Even teen relationships that start with a "Yes," eventually end with a "No." High school romances rarely last, and the few that do still have occasional periods of separation. So, unless both partners agree to the split, one person inevitably gets dumped. If it happens to be your daughter, how well will she take it? Can she pick herself up and move on, or will she wallow in denial and self-pity? You can get a good sense of her resiliency by looking back at how she has responded to past disappointments. Maybe she didn't make the starting rotation on the volleyball team or earn first chair in the school band. Disappointing outcomes for sure, but certainly not devastating events worth weeks of angst, tears, and anger. Rejection is always difficult, but it doesn't have to be debilitating. As a parent, you can help your daughter learn how to deal with relationship rejection by looking at the big picture:

- **Assess her role.** Examine any behaviors that may have contributed to the outcome. Is there anything she could have done differently to avoid the negative result?

- **Assess the situation.** Review the expectations she had as well as the role others played in the relationship. Was there too much pressure, too little in common, or had the relationship simply run its course? Sometimes, no one person or one event is to blame.

- **Seek support.** It's hard to dwell on negative feelings if you surround yourself with friends and family who care about you.

- **Focus on the future.** No matter what issues led to one breakup, it doesn't mean the next one is doomed, too. Help your daughter identify the good and bad aspects of the relationship, and remind her that the lessons she learns will make her a better person in her next dating relationship.

We started this chapter by asking you how you would decide when your daughter is ready for dating. As you can see, it involves more thought than circling a date on a calendar. Past behavior, social skills, and emotional maturity are important considerations. So if you were looking for us to give you a specific age, we can't. That answer is for you and your daughter to decide. The trick, of course, is coming to an agreement on when she's ready for group dating and solo dating.

Using Rationales to Support Rules

We've given our view on why we think your daughter, if she's in junior high, should not be pairing off and dating someone exclusively. But rather than simply say junior high dating is unnecessary and leave it at that, we tried to point out the potential problems. We wanted you to know the reasons behind our opinion. And we suggested an alternative. Rather than tell you never to use calendar age when deciding when your daughter should start dating, we explained the benefits of looking at her emotional maturity and social skills. When you talk to your daughter about your family's dating rules, you have to provide her with rationales for why the rules are necessary. Simply making rules for the sake of having rules doesn't work. Your daughter needs to know the "why" behind each rule.

Rationales connect an individual's actions to the consequences of those actions. If your daughter understands the benefits of a specific rule, she is more likely to follow that rule in the future. Although rationales alone won't guarantee compliance, using them has several benefits:

- **They help make your daughter see you as someone who is fair.** When your daughter hears a rationale, she is likely to understand that what you are saying has relevance. The rationale helps her know that you are addressing an issue or behavior that is going to help her. It's not a personal attack on her character.

- **They aid in moral development.** When you point out how a person's behavior affects others, you are helping your daughter become more self-reflective and other-centered.

- **They build a positive relationship.** When you give rationales, your daughter sees that you care. Creating any type of family rule is easier when a positive relationship exists between parent and child.

There are three different kinds of reasons you can give your daughter for why a rule is important. The type of reason you use will depend on what you think will help her the most. The reasons can describe potential benefits to your daughter, possible negative outcomes, or benefits to others.

Benefits to self. Use this rationale when you want your daughter to see how a rule will affect her. It might sound something like this: "If you go to the dance with a group instead of with a date, you can dance with whomever you choose, and you won't feel like you're stuck."

Negative outcomes. When you use this type of rationale, you are pointing out an undesirable outcome for her actions. Here is how one parent explained why he didn't want his daughter to spend all her free time with her boyfriend: "When you focus all your attention on him, your friends feel ignored and unimportant. If they feel that way, you'll lose your girlfriends."

Concern for others. This type of rationale puts your daughter in someone else's shoes. This is a good way to help her see a situation from another point of view, and gives her an opportunity to think about how she might feel if someone acted a certain way toward her. An example of this kind of rationale was used by a parent who didn't want her daughter being affectionate toward her boyfriend. She said, "Your little sisters look up to you and want to do everything you do. How can we teach them about healthy boundaries if they see you kissing and hanging on your boyfriend?"

As we look at other dating rules in the following chapters, we'll suggest rationales that can help your daughter understand why certain rules are necessary. Realize, though, that rationales alone seldom are enough to change behavior or influence your daughter's decision to follow a rule. Rationales have to be coupled with consequences and conversations in which you teach your daughter about dating skills and values.

Age-Appropriate Relationships

Deciding when your daughter is mature enough for a dating relationship is only half the equation. What about the age of her dates? As a general rule, we tell parents that if they have a child in junior high, that child shouldn't get involved with someone in high school. If the child is in high school, he or she shouldn't be involved with anyone in junior high or college. From that rule, we add a second: Teen dating couples should have no more than a two-year age difference. For young girls, hooking up with older guys can have serious consequences:

- Relationships with significantly older partners are much more likely to be sexual than relationships with someone who is slightly older, the same age, or slightly younger.

- One in six girls who had voluntary sex at age 14 or younger say their first partner was five or more years older.

- More than one in 10 girls who first had sex before age 15 described the experience as non-voluntary and many more described it as relatively unwanted.

- Sexually experienced youth between the ages of 12 and 14 are much more likely to engage in other risky behaviors, such as smoking, drinking, and using drugs.

Source: *14 and Younger: The Sexual Behavior of Young Adolescents (Summary)*. National Campaign to Prevent Teen Pregnancy

Turn to the "Are You Dateable?" exercise on page 179 for a simple way to ask your daughter about her dating readiness.

Chapter 4

A Roadmap for Safe Dating

or Fasten Your Belts... It's Date Night

"Watching your daughter being collected by her date feels like handing over a million dollar Stradivarius to a gorilla."

– JIM BISHOP, AMERICAN WRITER

When a young man knocks on your door, or worse, honks from his car in the driveway, and your daughter jets out on a date, do you feel like Mr. Bishop? Plenty of parents do. One father we know makes sure that his daughter's gentleman callers never leave his premises without knowing how precious their date is. Nonchalantly, the father will say, "I value my home, and I would never allow anyone to misuse it or tear it up." After slow nods of understanding from the boy, the father continues, "I value my daughter way more than this house. If you take her out, you better not tear her up. Do you hear me?" The young lad nods a fast and furious "Yes" – if he's smart. This dad wants his warning to be the last words ringing in the young man's ears when he leaves and the first words he remembers – in the car, on the dance floor, at the restaurant, or in the theater. Whatever the couple does, Dad hopes his parting words will squash any devious or mischievous ideas the two might entertain over the course of the evening. The implied threat of severe consequences is his insurance policy to protect against any inappropriate behaviors. He trusts his daughter enough to date; he doesn't necessarily trust that the boy will be a good influence.

When you allow your daughter to date, you have some confidence in her ability to make good choices. If you didn't, she wouldn't be dating. However, no matter how much trust you give your daughter, or how much fear you put into her date, watching her get into a car with a teenage boy at the wheel is enough to make anyone double over with anxiety. In this chapter, we examine what it takes to make a date safe and fun for kids and less nerve-racking for parents.

Every Date Needs a Plan

There are many things to consider and discuss with your daughter before she accepts a date or you agree she can go out. First, and most important, what is the plan? Your daughter should be able to answer these basic questions:

- Who is she going with?
- Where are they going?
- How are they getting there (who's driving)?
- What will they be doing?

Get Your Motor Runnin'

When I was 16, I accepted a date from "Kyle." Because he was a new guy in my life, my parents insisted on meeting him. When he came to pick me up, Mom, Dad and all seven of my brothers gathered in the living room to say "Hello." Before Kyle even had a chance to ring the doorbell, my parents swung open the front door and ushered him inside. He looked scared, and I know my brothers intimidated him. After quick introductions and uncomfortable chit-chat, we were free to go. We should have stayed home.

When Kyle tried to start his car, the motor moaned. He gave me a sheepish grin and turned the key a second time. Again, it would not start. Kyle popped the hood and yelled back at me that the alternator was bad. He said he was going to "bump start" it – get the car rolling and let out the clutch quickly so the engine could turn over. I offered to help, but he insisted on doing it himself. After three failed attempts of pushing and jumping, Kyle was exhausted and sweaty. As he got ready to try one more time, out marched all my brothers. Kyle look mortified as my brothers surrounded him and started pushing. Thank goodness they came because they got the car started and we could go to dinner. The meal was okay, but we had a stomach-churning moment in the parking lot. As we were leaving, Kyle backed into a Mercedes, breaking its taillight. After he exchanged information with the angry driver, Kyle insisted we continue on our date and see a movie. He thought a good flick would get our minds off everything that happened. It almost worked. After the movie, we got in his car and, par for the evening, it would not start. This time it was the battery. Kyle left me in the car for what seemed like an eternity while he went for help. Eventually a stranger came and jumped the battery. On the way home, I started laughing because the whole evening seemed to be one disaster after another. Kyle didn't see the humor, and he didn't ask me out again.

– A Lemon for a Date

- When will she be home?
- How can she be reached in case of an emergency (phone number, address, etc.)?

Before your daughter accepts an offer for a date, she should at least know who she's going with and where she's going. And before you agree to let her go out, you should know that information, too. If she can't tell you what the plan is, your answer should be "No." Even if your daughter has already dated, and things turned out okay in the past, don't assume there's no need to question the present. Any time your teen is unsure or deliberately vague about a date, be cautious. She could be trying to hide her true intentions, knowing that you would disapprove and possibly not allow her to go out.

As a parent, you should want to know who your daughter dates, where they go, and what they do, if for no other reason than simple safety. If your daughter and her companion know that you can check on their activities, either by calling them, speaking to their friends, or hearing gossip on the "parent grapevine," they will be less inclined to try to pull something over on you. If you find out your daughter wasn't where she said she would be, or wasn't with who she said she would be with, find out why. Maybe there's an innocent explanation. Unexpected events can sometimes cause a change in plans. However, your daughter should understand that she has a responsibility to call and let you know of any changes. If there is no good explanation for why she told you one thing, but did another, she should face consequences that will deter her from trying to intentionally deceive you again.

Sometimes, parents tell us their daughters don't appreciate getting the fifth degree every time they want to go on a date. These teens, who think of themselves as "practically adult," complain that their parents don't trust them or are being too protective. You may hear similar complaints from your teen. But the rationales, or reasons, for why parents need to ask questions mainly involve safety and common courtesy. What if there is a family emergency involving a parent, grandparent, or sibling, and your daughter needs to rush home or to a hospital? If you don't know where she is or how to reach her, an already difficult situation can become desperate. Disappearing into some black hole is irresponsible. On the flip side, you want your daughter to know how and where to reach you if something should happen to her or her date. The truly adult perspective is knowing that emergencies can happen, and everyone has an obligation to the family, not just themselves.

Rules for the Road

After your daughter fills you in on the who, what, where, and when of a date, it's your turn to review the family dating policy. If the date involves a teen driver, and most usually do, some special advice may be necessary. Here are a few common-sense rules or guidelines that you may want to consider and discuss as your daughter prepares for her date:

No honking, then dashing.

If your daughter is about to step out with a young man you've never met, the date shouldn't start until proper introductions are made. That means he can't sit in the driveway honking the horn until your daughter dashes out. A good first rule for the evening is that he comes to the door, steps inside, and introduces himself. It would also be nice if your daughter informs her dates of this rule before they show up at your house. That way they won't feel like they're being ambushed. Obviously, you'll be curious to know what kind of boy your daughter is dating and what kind of family he comes from. You might break the ice by asking what his parents do for a living, if he has any siblings, or how he likes his car. But beyond satisfying your own curiosities, there are other benefits to meeting face to face with your daughter's date:

> "Any man who can drive safely while kissing a pretty girl is simply not giving the kiss the attention it deserves."
>
> – ALBERT EINSTEIN
> RENOWNED PHYSICIST

- You can ask him about the plans for the evening. Does what he tells you match what your daughter told you? If not, why not?

- You can check to see if he's impaired. If he tries to avoid meeting you or resists the idea, is he trying to hide something? Are his eyes glassy or bloodshot? Does he have the odor of alcohol or cigarette smoke? There may be a reasonable explanation for odd behaviors (nervousness) or unusual appearance (illness). But if he doesn't bother to come to the door, how are you going to know if he's someone you want your daughter to leave with?

- You can remind him that your daughter doesn't

exist in a vacuum, but rather comes from a caring family. If he sees she is surrounded by people who care for her and how she's treated, he will get the message that he is accountable and responsible for her well-being.

Should you demand that your daughter's dates come to the door every time, even on the third, fourth, or fifth date? Probably not. While it may be nice, that kind of insistence can be overbearing, if not impractical. If you don't have any reason to be concerned and the date has earned your trust, then periodic chats with your daughter about how things are going and the occasional drop-in from a boy she's gone out with several times before may be all the reassurance you need.

Know your local and state driving laws.

Being aware of your community's regulations regarding teen drivers can guide the dating rules you have in your family, including curfew. For example, many states use graduated driving permits for young drivers. These permits have certain restrictions that are advantageous to parents. A common restriction for teens with permits is that they cannot operate a motor vehicle after midnight unless a fully licensed driver (adult) is in the car. In Omaha, Nebraska, we know many parents who use that ordinance as their rationale for setting a midnight curfew on Friday and Saturday nights. Curfew issues that used to cause nasty squabbles between parents and teens are no longer so contentious because kids know their curfew is not some arbitrary parental decree, but an actual law whose violators face steep fines and other undesirable consequences.

A midnight curfew may be reasonable in many families on the weekend, but not so reasonable during the week. When your teen has school the next day, and you have to be at work early in the morning, a midnight curfew can create madness. Most families need different rules on weekends and weeknights. However, the motor vehicle laws that are such a good rationale for midnight curfews on Fridays and Saturdays don't hold the same appeal for parents on Tuesdays and Wednesdays. As a family, this is a good time to revisit the issue of balance. Remember what we said about clarifying priorities for your daughter? When her main responsibilities are to be a good student and member of the family, then decisions about curfews, and how often – if at all – she can date on weeknights, should be made from that point of view. Will she be able to complete her homework? Will she have enough time to study? Will she have time for family activities? Any decisions your family makes regarding dating rules should be guided by the larger goal of helping your teen achieve a healthy balance in her family life, academic life, and social life. Also, rules can be revisited. If there are problems, more restrictions may be necessary. Likewise, if behavior improves or goals are met, greater freedoms can be granted.

The family who owns the car, drives the car.

If your daughter's date involves using a car that is registered to her or someone else in the family, it's a good idea to remind her that no one else but her is to get behind the wheel unless it's an absolute emergency. If a teen turns the keys over to a friend, and the friend is involved in a personal-injury or property-damage accident, the resulting financial and legal mess can entangle everyone and destroy friendships. Another good rule of thumb for when your daughter is driving is to limit the number of passengers traveling with her. A car with only four seat belts should not be filled with six friends. Statistics show that teen drivers have a much greater risk for accidents when they have other teen passengers. Another safety precaution is to make sure your daughter's car is in good shape for road conditions. Windows and mirrors should be clean. The headlights should work. Tires should be properly inflated. The interior should be properly maintained, too. Empty bottles and cans left under the driver's seat can roll around, sometimes lodging under a brake or gas pedal, causing accidents. Remember, dating is a privilege, not a right. Properly maintaining the vehicle is another contingency, just like maintaining good grades, you can use when deciding if your daughter is responsible enough to date.

Trick or Treat?

When I was in high school, I was into the punk rock scene. My taste in guys matched my taste in music. One night my date arrived wearing a leather jacket with a silver chain strapped across his chest. His hair was dyed red and spiked, kind of like the American flag. My father opened the door, took one look at him, and said, "What Halloween character are you supposed to be?" Then Dad slammed the door shut. Needless to say, I did not leave the house that night!

– Rebel Without a Date

Good Dates Gone Bad

When girls describe to us their good dates gone bad, one of the most common situations involves ending up at a house party where there are no parents and the beer and debauchery are flowing freely. When their dates have the car keys in their pockets and beers in their hands, girls are put in a very vulnerable position. Is he going to be okay to drive? Should I drive? Maybe I can find a ride home with someone who hasn't been drinking? These are the questions girls have to grapple with, provided their judgment hasn't been impaired by the libations they might have enjoyed. Bad things are more likely to happen when teens find themselves in a house with no parents. That's why having a rule, such as, "*Home Alone* is a movie, not a plan for a date," is such a good idea. Sometimes, girls end up in these predicaments through no fault of their own. Other times, they knew exactly what they were doing, but thought they could handle it. If your daughter finds herself in a similar circumstance, what can she do? (We'll talk about the importance of having an escape plan in the next section.)

A big, unsupervised house party presents obvious problems. But a private party of two can be just as troublesome. When a teenage couple stays home alone, sexual temptation can be very real. It's tempting enough for adults, and even more so for teens who think and feel in the moment. Here is a cautionary tale one couple shared with us. They were fortunate, yet they were left feeling forlorn:

It was a late Saturday afternoon when the parents told their 15-year-old daughter they were going out for the evening. They had a club meeting that would last about an

Who's Holding the Keys?

On weekends, our daughter has a midnight curfew. She's a responsible girl who either makes it home early or just a few minutes late. So, when she missed curfew by 20 minutes one Sunday morning, after a night out with her boyfriend, we were a little concerned. We called her cell phone, hoping that she would tell us she was on her way home. But she didn't answer our call. At 1 a.m., she still wasn't home, and we became frantic. We tried calling her boyfriend's cell phone. No answer. Feeling more desperate, we called his mother – waking her up – to see if they were there. They weren't. Now, all the parents were in a panic. We tried calling their friends, hoping someone knew where they were. No one did.

We were getting ready to dial the police when finally, at 1:45 in the morning, the phone rang. It was our daughter, and she was fine. She said she had the left the keys in her unlocked car, but when her boyfriend went out to retrieve something earlier in the night, he locked the doors, not knowing the keys were inside. Neither of them could call home because their cell phones were locked inside, too. Luckily, our daughter remembered we had given her a motor club card, which happened to be in her purse along with some loose change. She and her date walked more than a mile to find a pay phone. Between the two of them, they only had enough coins to make one call, so our daughter called the motor club – instead of us! When we reminded her that we had an extra set of keys and could have picked her up much sooner, she was totally embarrassed. It never occurred to her to call home for help.

– Panicked Parent

hour, then they were going to grab a bite to eat. Thinking her parents would be gone for much of the evening, the daughter invited her boyfriend over. She didn't bother to ask if that was okay. But since she thought it might be an issue, she told her boyfriend not to park in the driveway. The young man parked his car on a side street behind the house so no neighbors would notice. The teens thought they were clever. However, when the parents left their club meeting, they decided they weren't that hungry. Rather than go to a restaurant, they headed home. When the parents walked into the house, the dad noticed someone's shadow in the backyard. Thinking it was his daughter enjoying their new gazebo and Jacuzzi, he went outside. When he rounded the corner of the gazebo, he found his daughter and her boyfriend in a naked embrace in the Jacuzzi. Stunned, all three froze for a moment. Then the dad looked at the boy and said, "You better put your clothes on and leave now." Mom and Dad were devastated. Their daughter was humiliated. At school on Monday, everyone heard about the Saturday night escapade. The boyfriend, an 18-year-old senior, never spoke to their daughter again, but he blabbed the story countless times to his buddies.

Would this teenage couple have gotten so cozy if they knew her parents were home? Of course not. But it never occurred to the parents that their daughter would invite her boyfriend over for a soak in the Jacuzzi, whether they were at home or not. Sometimes, teens have to be reminded that certain areas of the home are off limits to their dates, even when a parent is around. One room that should always be off limits to your daughter's dates or boyfriends is her bedroom. The whole idea about maintaining healthy boundaries and staying safe is to avoid dangerous situations. What does a bedroom imply? There's a sexual connotation for sure. But more than that, your daughter's bedroom is where she sleeps, changes clothes, writes in her journal, and puts on makeup. It is perhaps her most intimate place. Does her date need to see or do anything in her bedroom? Not really. Similarly, you shouldn't want her dates wandering through your bedroom or private bath. Every home has some area that's considered private family space. Reminding your daughter to honor the family's privacy, and the privacy of others when she's a guest in their homes, is a good thing.

Intimate situations, whether it involves a teenage couple sitting on a couch in the living room of an empty house or sitting in the front seat of a parked Mustang on a deserted street, can invite sexual intimacy. But is it enough to have a family rule that says your daughter can't be home alone with her boyfriend, or in any other private place without some adult presence, to keep it from ever happening? Maybe not. There is only so much policing you can do as a parent. However, you don't have to make it any easier for your teen to break the rules. For example, if you're going out for the evening, be somewhat ambiguous about your plans. Let your teen know you'll be checking in, and that you may or may not be home early. Your teen will think twice before getting a party started if she doesn't know when Mom or Dad might walk through the door. And if you say it's okay for your daughter to have friends over, then you or another adult should be home to greet them. If your daughter leaves and says she's going to be at Derrick's house until 11, you have every right to call his parents to confirm your daughter's plan and make sure it's okay for her to be there.

Some of the rules you make and precautions you take will probably be met with some resistance, maybe even anger, from your daughter. When that happens, and it most likely will, be honest. You're doing these things because you love her and care about her safety, not because you think she's an idiot or simply naïve. Tell her you know she's angry with you, and that's okay. You have to be her parent, not her go-along-with-anything best friend.

Mapping an Escape Route

If your daughter finds herself on a date with a young man who puts her in a dangerous environment, such as an underage drinking party, or creates a danger by driving erratically, acting sexually aggressive, or doing anything illegal, will she know how to get herself out of the situation safely? Of all the dating boundaries or rules you have for your family, nothing is more important than preparing your daughter for when a good date goes bad. Here are some guidelines to consider when creating an escape plan for your daughter:

Define a bad date.

The kind of bad date we're talking about doesn't involve a boy with bad breath or body odor. This is a date that threatens your daughter's well-being. Sometimes, kids can get so caught up in the moment, they don't realize the seriousness of the situation. For example, your daughter may think it's okay to go to a beer party, just as long as she doesn't take a sip. But does she realize that if the party gets busted, she's just as likely to be charged with being a minor in possession as those holding a beer? And if that happens, does she know she likely will be suspended or expelled from school activities? And what if her date drinks? She needs to know that he's not safe to be around because his inhibitions are lowered and his judgment is impaired.

Carry a cell phone.

If your teen has a cell phone, she should always take it with her on a date. If she doesn't have one, she should borrow yours or a friend's. If a cell phone is not an option, then she should always take along a pre-paid phone card or spare change so she can call for help if necessary.

Create a call list.

This is a list of approved adults who care about your daughter – a grandparent, youth minister, your daughter's best friend's mother, trusted neighbor, or close relative – and would drop everything to go get her. Sometimes, the fear of disappointing or angering a parent can outweigh any other safety considerations, and kids will stay in dangerous situations, and even dangerous relationships. Letting your daughter know there are "others" she can reach out to gives her another option when she's too embarrassed or scared to ask you for help. You don't want your daughter to feel trapped, like this teen we met at one of our workshops:

Seventeen-year-old Keilani had been in an exclusive dating relationship for almost two months. One evening, her boyfriend took her to his best friend's home. When they arrived, several other teens had gathered there and were drinking. The parents were not home.

Keilani's boyfriend grabbed a beer and offered her one, but she declined. Later in the evening, Keilani's boyfriend asked her to go with him for a walk on the golf course behind the house. It was very dark, and Keilani suspected it might be an invitation to something sexual. She replied, "No." Much to her surprise, he got angry, called her a slut, and shoved her hard. Keilani fell backwards and hit her head on an oak table. Sprawled on the floor, she was bleeding from a cut above her left eye. Immediately her boyfriend told her it was an accident and that he didn't mean it. Keilani found a friend and asked her to take her home.

She didn't know how to disguise or explain the cut. She couldn't tell her parents that she was at a beer party or in a house with no adult supervision, because that was against the family rules. She decided to lie and told her parents she slipped and fell down the stairs. Too afraid to talk to her parents, she was stuck.

Had Keilani's parents known her boyfriend was abusive, they could have stepped in to help her end the relationship immediately. But they had no clue. Keilani told us she wished she had had a call list when the incident happened. Most kids don't want to disappoint their parents. Just know-

---

Teens on the Road

Teens are the least experienced drivers on our roadways, which may explain some of these sobering statistics:

- 14% of all traffic deaths involve a teenage driver.
- More than half of all fatal accidents involving teens occur on weekends.
- Teen drivers killed in motor vehicle accidents had at least one youth passenger 45% of the time.
- More than one-third of deadly teen-driving accidents are speed-related.
- Teens make up 7% of licensed drivers but account for 14% of fatalities and 20% of all reported accidents.

Source: www.drivehomesafe.com

---

ing they can talk to someone else first, even when they know what they say will get back to their parents, makes it somehow easier to be honest.

Have a Healthy Curiosity

There's a smart way for good dates to begin, and it has little to do with the manner in which your daughter is "collected" by her date. A good date starts in the home with a conversation between you and your daughter. Ask your daughter the same questions she should ask a potential date before agreeing to go out: Where are we going? What will we be doing? Who will we be with? When will we be home?

Understanding what the plan is prepares you, as well as your daughter, for the date. Use the conversation to remind her about your expectations and answer any concerns she has, whether it's as benign as which fork to use at dinner or as serious as how to stop a sexual advance.

There's also a nice way for dates to end, and it has little to do with the manner in which your daughter is "returned" by her date. Waiting up for your daughter and talking to her about how the date went can be a positive way of bringing closure to the whole experience. A simple "How did things go?" or "Was it as much fun as you thought it would be?" can encourage her to share with you. It's also a way to show her you care.

The more open you are with your teen and the more you engage her in conversations, the more approachable you will seem. You want her to know that she can talk to you about anything. Let her know that no matter what happens, you love her and she can always come home. But getting your daughter to believe that requires you to repeat the message over and over again. You also have to show it in your actions. When she breaks a rule or gets into trouble, you can't go ballistic by yelling and immediately blaming her. Doing that may only scare her into silence and make her believe that she can't come to you again when she has a problem. But how do you stay calm when all you really want to do is explode? Try practicing a calming-down strategy, such as deep breathing, before your daughter comes to you with her troubles. Appearing calm can be difficult, but you only have to look under control on the outside. Later, you can vent the frustration and anger you felt to a spouse or anyone else who will listen.

In this chapter and the ones that follow, we talk about setting boundaries and rules to protect teens so they have happier dating experiences. The stories we share and the issues we discuss are meant to remind parents of the potential consequences of turning a blind eye to the whole teen dating scene. At the same time, parents who become so paranoid that they see threats – real and imagined – in every conceivable situation aren't doing their kids any favors either. Putting extreme restrictions on dating for no logical reason or assuming your teen is always up to no good creates a recipe for rebellion. In that environment, some teens will intentionally flaunt the rules out of pure spite. Having a healthy curiosity avoids both extremes. Parents should maintain a reasonable awareness of their teen's dating relationships by asking questions, listening, and observing behaviors. But they shouldn't impose themselves so aggressively that it becomes impossible for their teen to have any independence or life.

 Begin a family discussion about safe dating by doing the "Good Date? Bad Date?" exercise on page 186.

Chapter 5

Addressing Dressing

Modesty Is Always in Style

"'Are you a mom?' asked an infectiously bubbly teen, her quizzical expression reflecting at me from the full-length mirror in front of her. What a peculiar question, I thought, to ask a stranger in the middle of a dress shop's changing room. I responded, 'Yes, I have two daughters. Why do you ask?' 'What do you think of this?' the teen said as she twirled around to show me the dress she was sporting. In the quiet recesses of my mind, I screamed, 'That dress makes you look like a two-dollar hooker!' After reflecting for a moment, I smiled and voiced the most appropriate response I could: 'What is the event, and what will you be doing?'"

The mother who had this experience in the dress shop told us that the girl looked like she had been vacuum-sealed inside the dress. The short, strapless number was not flattering to her figure, as every bulge and blemish was plainly visible. Despite what the mom thought was obviously a fashion faux pas, the girl's friends were telling her she looked fine, the dress was "too cute," and she would look great with her hair in an updo. Her friends, like many teenage girls, apparently buy into the old adage that "less is more," especially when it concerns their clothing choices. Whether it's necklines that plunge to the navel or skirts with slits that seemingly never stop, skin is the new must-have accessory. But what effect is this fashion trend having on teen relationships?

The Guy's Perspective

When we ask teenage boys what they think when they see girls at school or the mall dressed in the provocative styles made popular by trendy celebrities such as Christina Aguilera, Pink, or Paris Hilton, the response is almost universal: She wants IT. By "it," the boys don't mean attention, although the provocatively dressed girls certainly draw the stares and snickers of these young men. The boys' definition of "it" is sex or sexual attention. Many also believe the girls want guys to see them as sexy. Granted, most boys definitely like seeing bare midriffs, short shorts, and tiny tops. But if you recall from Chapter 2, the male brain is wired differently. Guys can be aroused, much more so than girls, by visual stimulation alone. They will undress girls with their eyes, which doesn't take much effort when the girls are flaunting or flashing their assets. Yet many adolescent girls we talk to are surprised that a guy would have sexual thoughts just from looking at how they're dressed. That point was made abundantly clear to a father who shared his experience with us:

His daughter, Taysha, was a member of the high school varsity swim team. At the first co-ed meet of the season, he noticed her engaging in behavior that troubled him. After each event she swam, Taysha emerged from the pool and hugged all her teammates, including the boys. Just an innocent gesture of excitement and team unity? That's what his daughter thought. But Dad was shocked to see his wet, scantily clad girl getting bear hugs from wet young men wearing skin-tight Speedos. When Taysha came home from the meet, her father asked her why she let the boys hug her like that. She looked at him like he was crazy. She had no idea what he was implying. Of course, Dad was remembering his own youth. What Taysha saw as a gesture of support, her father saw as an opportunistic moment for a young man to cop a feel. Taysha was adamant that there was nothing sexual about the hugs. For one thing, she said she wasn't thinking about sex; they were just hugs. Dad reminded her that she wasn't the only one in the embrace, and her hugs could be easily misinterpreted to mean something other than "Good job!" He told Taysha the next time she climbed out of the pool, he wanted to see her give high-fives and handshakes, not hugs.

Now you might agree with Taysha that in the context of a high school swim meet, the hugs were innocent. They may very well have been. But Dad didn't want his daughter's hugs to become sexual fantasies for the boys. He wanted her to know that body language has meaning and can be misinterpreted. It was a good lesson on appropriate physical boundaries and one that many teens learn too late. Have you ever seen girls sitting on their boyfriends' laps, stroking their legs, or a group of kids piled in front of the television with their legs and arms intertwined with one another? These are situations that can elicit sexual thoughts and feelings. It's natural for teens to think about sex, but they can make it nearly impossible to think about anything else because of how they dress, what they say, and what they do.

When it comes to dating, girls like to look like runway models. That means many choose fashion over function. The problem, however, is that some girls seem more concerned about impressing other girls with their cutting-edge clothes than the impression they're making on the boys they're actually dating. They don't realize the level of sexual flirtation and attraction they can generate when their dates see lots of skin. Girls say they want to be treated with respect, but when they wear outfits that draw attention to their breasts or butts, guys get a mixed, murky message. We've actually had adolescent boys ask us how they should respond to their dates when they dress with little modesty. Here are a few of the questions young males have running through their heads:

- What am I supposed to look at?
- What does she want from me?
- Does she want me to comment on her body?
- Does she want me to make a pass at her?
- How am I supposed to act?

Guys don't really know what their dates' expectations are, and many are too intimidated or insecure to ask. The whole dating situation is confusing enough, filled with lots of ambiguity. As a parent, do you want your daughter to make the date any harder than it already is?

The Girl's Perspective

If your daughter pressures you to buy or has bought herself clothing you consider to be inappropriate, tell her why you feel that choice is wrong for her. She might argue that everyone wears that style or that guys only pay attention to girls who dress a certain way. All valid points. But as a parent, you should point out that people can draw attention to themselves in lots of different ways, some of which are not good or healthy. Help her to understand that what she wears communicates a message, whether she likes it or not or agrees with the message or not. A good question to ask is what she thinks when she sees girls dressed provocatively, whether it's thong panties peaking out from low-rise designer jeans or skimpy shorts that show some of their backside. Most teen girls give us the same answer as the boys: She wants "IT."

One father we met was determined to keep his teen daughters from looking like sex kittens. In the mornings, he stood at the foot of the stairs so he could see what his girls were wearing before they walked out the door to school. If he didn't approve of their attire, he marched them back up the steps to change clothes. He did the same thing on date night. It wasn't a perfect method, as he sometimes caught his girls with a change of clothes in their backpacks or wearing second outfits underneath their Dad-approved clothes. Despite the games the girls occasionally played to get past their father's inspection, they knew he had limits. And they knew why he wanted them to look respectable, even if they didn't always agree with his definition. When your daughter is deciding how to dress for a date, what statement do you want her to make? Here are a few messages that always wear well:

Real confidence isn't found in designer labels.

How much freedom or confidence does a girl really have if she's constantly tugging at her dress straps or blouse, afraid she's about to have her own Janet Jackson moment? Today's teen marketers are quite savvy – and successful – at associating a sexualized style of dress with liberation and re-bellion. Adolescent girls have bought into the message that wearing tight, revealing clothes makes a "power" statement. Teens tell us that if a guy can't handle the way they dress, it's his problem, not theirs. That may be true. But most young girls who rely on skimpy clothes to attract dates lack the emotional intelligence and experience to deal with the many unwanted and unexpected stares, sneers, and sugges-tions that their provocative appearance attracts.

Comfort counts.

The mom in the dress shop gave a great response to the girl who stopped her and asked what she thought of her dress: "What's the event, and what will you be doing?" Some-times, girls can get so excited about their date or become so concerned about creating the perfect "look," they forget to think about what's appropriate for the activity. We've all seen the girl who comes to the Friday night football game in a mini-skirt and high heels. Not only does she look a little out of place, the cool autumn evening and steep bleacher seating conspire to make her cold and clumsy. Dressing ap-propriately for the occasion, whatever it may be, is a skill that every child should learn.

Modesty shows, and attracts, respect.

Time and time again girls tell us they wish guys would treat them with more respect. Most say they want guys to see them for who they are on the inside instead of judging them by how they look on the outside. That's a great attitude, and one you want your daughter to have. To help her earn the respect she deserves, make her mindful of body language. If she really wants people to appreciate her personality, values, and interests, she shouldn't distract them by emphasizing only her body or bare skin. A modest style of dress (no spaghetti straps, bare midriffs, backless dresses, mini-mini skirts, stiletto heels, etc.) can go a long way in helping people see her as something other than a sexual object. In addition to appearance, she should think about her behaviors and activities. If she hangs all over guys, makes suggestive comments, or allows boyfriends to call her derisive names, such as "skank" or "ho," she'll earn the amount of respect her behavior suggests she wants – not much.

The Mother of All Dates – Prom

When it comes to attire, nothing can create a rift between parents and their daughters quite like that annual rite of passage – prom. There's nothing like a high school formal to push every possible dating issue to the forefront, sending everyone into hysterics as they search for perfection – the perfect dress, the perfect date, the perfect hair, the perfect shoes, the perfect ride, the perfect dinner, the perfect after party, etc. Girls can obsess (for months) over finding a one-of-a-kind dress, with accessories to match everything from their hair to their heels. Boys can work hard to find dates, and once found, worry how they're going to "pimp their ride" (arrive in a regular limo or stretch SUV?). Teens focus on the details that matter to them. It's the parents who are left to deal with the fallout when the expenses and expectations soar beyond what's reasonable or attainable.

Prom is a billion-dollar industry because marketers, teens, and many parents have given this high school dance the same reverence as a wedding, with a price tag to match. There are Web sites and magazines devoted entirely to "helping" teens experience the "ideal" prom. One online site, selling couture gowns and accessories, had this message for teens: "Remember to start saving early, because going to prom is not cheap. Your memories will last a lifetime so don't skimp on the things that are most important to you. You don't want to regret your decisions later. For the most part, there is only one prom." Sounds a lot like how one might describe a wedding, doesn't it? The same site also offered several "Do's and Don'ts in Prom Etiquette." The advice for the ladies included:[1]

- Do wear body glitter so you sparkle.
  (Message: Girls, again, should emphasize their bodies.)

- Don't leave your date to be with your friends the whole night. He has a lot of time invested in this night, make it special.
  (Message: Girls "owe" their date something to make the night "special." Is it time? Is it a compliment? Is it a sexual favor? Is it another date? What message is implied, and what message is heard?)

- Don't make a scene, you'll mess up your makeup from crying.

(Message: Girls are too emotional and maybe they should think twice before objecting to a bad idea, behavior, or situation.)

• Do make sure that you thank your date for dinner, IF it was good!
(Message: Politeness is a choice that is dependent on personal whims, not a virtue worth practicing regardless of the circumstances.)

Big Night, Bright Light

I was so excited when my daughter told me she had been asked to her first prom that I went and bought a video camera. For posterity's sake, I hoped to capture as much of the special evening as she would let me. I had goose bumps just thinking about her watching the video with her own kids some day. What would they think watching their mom go off on her first big date? Unfortunately, I gave more thought to the future than the present. When my daughter's date arrived, we went out to the backyard so I could use the spring foliage as a backdrop. The young man was very accommodating, and I didn't embarrass my daughter too much.

Right after they left for the evening, I went inside and popped the tape into the VCR. What came up on the screen wasn't what I had hoped to see. Instead of watching my daughter and her handsome gentleman, all I saw was a bright white light. All the footage I shot outside was taken looking into the sun. The entire tape consisted of faceless voices coming from a blinding white light.

— BUMMED MOM

To be fair, several of the do's and don'ts focused on table manners and how to be courteous. But some of the advice, like much of the site itself, reflected the consumerism (a "don't" for guys was "forget your cash") and vanity (another "don't" for guys was "forget to tell her how beautiful she looks") that defines the modern prom. The indulgence and wanton behavior this dance elicits from teens and parents was too much for one principal. He canceled his school's prom. In a letter to parents, the principal explained his reasoning: "It is not primarily the sex/booze/drugs that surround this event, as problematic as they might be; it is rather the flaunting of affluence, assuming exaggerated expenses, a pursuit of vanity for vanity's sake – in a word, financial decadence."[2]

Maybe you know parents who spring for luxury limos and other perks for their children's prom. Maybe you know girls who spend several hundred, even a thousand, dollars for designer dresses. Maybe you've already lived through a daughter's prom and went along with her wishes in spite of your unease about its extravagance. Maybe you secretly hope your daughter's school will cancel prom so you won't have to deal with any of it. As appealing as that may sound, there will always be another prom, homecoming, winter formal, or spring fling to test your patience and your daughter's perspective. The good news is that there are a lot of things you can do to combat the crush of marketing and materialism.

Prom's Real Purpose

The whole purpose of prom, or any school-sponsored formal, is to give young people the chance to develop their social skills. Somehow that always gets forgotten. That's why it's important to remind your daughter that prom is really an opportunity for her to practice the social behaviors that will benefit her for the rest of her life. She needs to learn how to walk, talk, dress, and act appropriately in formal situations. The more you can help your daughter understand the purpose of prom, the less likely she is to inflate prom into something it was never meant to be. A good way to start your discussion is to ask, "What do you want to remember?" We've posed that question to hundreds of girls. While they all say they want to have fun and be "seen," most talk about wanting to remember their friends and not having any regrets. That's a great goal! Prom should be about social relationships, not social status. Here are tips to help your family keep things in perspective when it comes to prom's biggest issues:

The dress

We've met teens who started prepping for their proms as early as four months in advance. They scheduled tanning sessions and appointments for manicures and pedicures. And, of course, they dieted. They browsed magazines and hit the shops looking at dresses, shoes, earrings, and handbags. The time and effort these girls put into preparing their physical selves dwarfed anything their mothers did before their own weddings! All of this preparation costs money and heightens expectations. Can you imagine how disappointed these girls would be if they were not asked to prom? We've also met parents whose daughters, in teary-eyed tirades, pleaded for new dresses. But their pleas didn't come until days before the big event. These last-minute surprises often forced parents into on-the-spot purchases that were expensive ("Just buy it; we don't have time to find a deal") and regrettable ("It's so revealing, but that's the only style they have").

When it comes to your daughter's dress, here are a few do's and don'ts that can help tone down some of the extravagance and drama. By following these guidelines, you'll also help your daughter become a better consumer and a more grounded individual:

- **Don't be clueless about school-sponsored formals.** Be proactive and ask around when prom, homecoming, or other formals are scheduled. If it's a school-sponsored event, don't be afraid to call the school and find out if there's a dress code or other guidelines. You'll feel better because you'll know what's going on, and you can start talking to your daughter about her plans and clarifying expectations and rules for the evening.

- **Do set a limit on spending.** If your daughter needs a new dress, put a limit on how much she can spend. What's reasonable will depend somewhat on your family's financial resources. But you should encourage your daughter to think outside the box when dress shopping. There are other alternatives, often more affordable, than going to traditional department stores or boutiques. For example, many larger communities have vintage clothing stores that offer reasonable and distinctive choices. Other options worth considering with your daughter include having her swap last year's homecoming or prom dress with a friend's, making her own dress, or redesigning and altering an old dress to make it new and contemporary.

- **Do emphasize comfort, not sexiness.** When it comes to the dress, the overall goal should be to be fashionable, yet modest. If you're shopping with your daughter, you shouldn't be the one dictating all of the decisions. You should help her make the best choice she can. Think of the mom in the dress shop who was asked her opinion. She wanted to shout out how wrong the girl's dress was. But rather than say something that would make the girl feel awkward or bad, she asked questions that made the young lady think more critically about her choice. When your daughter is picking a dress, she should ask herself:
  - Can I dance in this dress?
  - Can I get in and out of the car comfortably in these clothes?
  - Will I spend the entire evening worrying that I might pop out of the dress?
  - Will my date's parents be embarrassed by how I'm dressed?

You don't want to be the clothing Nazi, but you do want to set some limits. You want to help your daughter look beyond the style or label and see the bigger picture. Help her to understand that if she wants to have a carefree evening with no regrets, her choices matter.

If you can't be with your daughter when she's shopping for a formal dress, most department stores will put items on hold for 24 hours at no cost. If she finds a dress, have her put it on hold until you have a chance to look it over. That's better than being uninvolved or turning over the family credit card and leaving her to the whims and tastes of friends and strangers.

The dinner

If your daughter saved money on her dress, maybe you won't mind if she and her date splurge on a four-course meal at a five-star restaurant. Besides, it's the guy who usually picks up the tab, right? Well even if your daughter isn't expected to pay, that doesn't mean you can't offer alternatives so the young man doesn't break the bank. Aside from not wanting him to go broke, there are other benefits that have much more to do with your daughter. Whenever a young man spends lavishly on a date, it can create a situation in which the girl feels guilty about his generosity. She may think she owes him something in return. Or, he may intentionally manipulate her into believing she has to provide some form of payback, be it another date, a kiss, or a favor. In healthy dating relationships, each individual shares power and no one is forced to feel obligated to the other. Let your teen know that she doesn't have to do anything just because a date spends lots of money or goes to extravagant lengths. He shouldn't use his choices to make her feel guilty.

On prom night, the dinner is one of the biggest highlights for most teens. Dressed to the nines, it's natural for them to want to enjoy a dining experience that is as fine as their fashions. For some, that means making reservations at restaurants where formal attire is expected, if not required. Those upscale eateries also require big wallets. That's not

The Pooch and the Pink Cake

A few weeks before prom, Darrick invited me to stop by his house after school. When I got there, he met me at the door and asked me to wait outside for a few minutes. I said okay, thinking he needed to straighten up or something. While I stood outside, I overheard him screaming at "someone" inside. A few minutes later he came back to the door and invited me in. Before I could ask him what the commotion was about, he told me to grab a couple sodas from the fridge. When I opened the refrigerator door, I saw a perfectly square pink cake with a big chunk missing from its center. It looked as if someone had taken a bare hand and clawed out a piece. The message on top of the cake read, "Will yo........om with me?"

Darrick explained that another friend of ours was helping him decorate the cake, which was how he was going to ask me to prom. When I arrived, the friend was supposed to put the cake in the fridge and go hide. She hid but didn't put the cake away. When Darrick went back to the kitchen to make sure everything was ready (which was why he asked me to wait outside), he found the family dog on the kitchen table eating his prom proposal! That's why I heard all the yelling, and why the cake was missing a chunk and the message was almost incomprehensible.

– STILL-LAUGHING PROM DATE

necessarily a bad thing, if kids keep things realistic. But sometimes, the fancier things get because of the money being spent, the more pressure kids feel to have a perfect experience. And because perfection is elusive, this often sets young people up for disappointment. To alleviate some of the stress and expense kids face on prom night, consider dining alternatives that require smaller budgets but are just as fun and rewarding. Here is one option that parents and teens have experimented with. It may appeal to your family, too. At the very least, it's a reminder that fine dining doesn't have to cost teens a fortune.

If your daughter is going with a group of friends, offer to host a pre-prom dinner at your home or another parent's home. Ask the other parents if they would like to help you prepare a special meal. You can get creative by having a theme or an elaborate table setting. There can be music, special appetizers, and exotic non-alcoholic beverages. The meal can be as fancy (grilled steak or smoked fish) or fun (nachos and pizza) as the kids want. Whatever the meal, it's likely to be less expensive and more filling than restaurant fare.

This dining option works best when parents stay mostly out of sight. They should occupy themselves in the kitchen, giving the kids their own space to eat, drink and be merry. Teens we talked to say they loved the home cooking, but what they really appreciated was the ease and comfort they felt. Most agreed it was more relaxing than sitting in a stuffy restaurant getting stared at by strangers. Even if this suggestion isn't appetizing to you or your teen, maybe it will spark a debate in your family on how to avoid unnecessary expenses or excessive spending on prom night.

The after party

Prom has traditionally been an evening where the party continues long after the music stops. In the not-so-distant past, prom-goers found ways to celebrate until sunrise. Unfortunately, much of what they did during those pre-dawn hours was dangerous, even deadly. In an effort to reduce reckless behavior, including drinking and driving, schools and communities banded together to give kids a safe, chaperoned alternative. Today, school- and parent-sponsored post-prom parties are the norm. Teens can celebrate into the early morning without many of the worries and dangers that previously existed. The parties are great for parents, too. They enjoy peace of mind knowing their children are in a healthy, supervised environment.

As wonderful as these after parties can be, they apparently aren't enough for some teens. An increasingly popular addition to the post-prom festivities is the coed sleepover. The logic behind these slumber parties eludes us. What purpose is there in having teenage guys and gals falling asleep together? Is it an effort to extend a long night of fun even further? The reasoning may be hard to understand, but the risks are not. Sleeping is a very vulnerable state. Why would parents want to create circumstances in which kids could be so easily taken advantage of? The dangers of sexual pranks, experimentation, even abuse, at these sleepovers exist regardless of how innocent teens claim them to be or how much supervision parents claim to provide. Kids and parents have enough worries on prom night without creating situations that invite trouble and confusion.

If your daughter tells you "everyone" is going somewhere after the dance and that it's okay with all the other kids' parents, pick up the phone and start asking around. Find out if they're really okay with the idea. What you're likely to hear from some parents is that they're going along with it because they don't want to be the only parents to say "No." Peer pressure can influence moms and dads just as much as their kids. If an idea like a coed sleepover makes you uneasy, you're probably not alone. Share your concerns with others, and say "No" together, or offer an alternative that's acceptable to everyone.

When it comes to prom, schools are getting much better at managing behaviors and toning down some of the outrageousness. Many have rules dealing with everything from appropriate dress to acceptable styles of dance. Find out what your school administrators are doing to ensure that prom continues to serve its original purpose. Their efforts can make a parent's job easier. Use the school's regulations as rationales for the decisions and limits you make about clothes, curfew, or the after party. If your daughter throws tantrums or makes demands that will blow prom way out of proportion, remember our advice from Chapter 3. If she can't have a reasonable response or accept "No" for an answer in a conversation about going to prom, then she probably doesn't have the skills or the maturity to be anyone's prom date.

Final Words

Author Wendy Shalit describes modesty as "a reflection of self-worth, of having such a high opinion of yourself that you don't need to boast or put your body on display for all to see."[3] In today's image-is-everything culture, modesty is a virtue lost. It's absent in girls who flaunt their bodies instead of their brains to impress guys. It's absent on prom nights that are remembered more for money and materialism than friends and relationships. It's absent from marketers who sell the idea that happiness, love, and success come from using a particular product or having a certain look. It's absent in teens who see dating as one big attention-seeking opportunity.

As parents, we need to offer a different message. We need to teach our daughters that beauty isn't just about the body. We need to tell our daughters that dating relationships are about making friendships, not using others. We need to help our daughters value people more than things. We need to show our daughters that modesty is never out of style for women with confidence and self-respect.

 Get creative when talking about appropriate attire and appearance by doing the "Fashionista Art Project" on page 188.

---

1 "Do's and Don'ts in Prom Etiquette," viewed at http://www.prom-dressshop.com/Promtips/PromDos.html, November 9, 2005.

2 Associated Press, "Long Island Principal Cancels Prom," viewed at http://www.cnn.com/2005/US/10/16/prom.canceled.ap/index.html, November 10, 2005.

3 Shalit, Wendy. *A Return to Modesty: Discovering the Lost Virtue.* New York: Free Press (1999) p. 132.

Chapter 6

Gift Giving

and Other Musings on Money Matters

*"I have a job, and I can buy whatever I want!
It's my money, and if I want something, I can
have it!" shouted 15-year-old Madison to her
parents after coming home with a new TV for her
bedroom. She had twice asked her parents for a
television, and twice her parents had said "No."
They didn't want her staying up all hours of the
night watching who knows what, nor did they
want her isolating herself in her room. Madison
hoped that by buying the tube with money she
had earned, her parents would be more agreeable.
They weren't. Seeing her defy their wishes, Madison's parents responded, "When you want to start
paying $300 a month in rent for the bedroom
we're providing you, then you can put whatever
you want in there. Until then, the answer is still,
'NO!'" The television set was returned to the elec-
tronics store the next day.*

Madison's rationale for buying a TV, in spite of her parents' objections, is one that many teens use to justify their spending: If I earn my own money, I can buy whatever I want. This argument gives some parents pause. Why shouldn't teens be allowed to make their own purchasing decisions if it's not costing Mom or Dad a penny? Chapter 5 exposed some of the consequences for parents and teens when possessions and money are valued more than people and relationships. But Madison's situation also shows how teens sometimes value things that aren't appropriate for their age or circumstance. When you combine the money that teens have at their disposal with their desire for consumption and instant gratification, all kinds of crazy and questionable purchases can be made. The same thing can happen in dating relationships.

Teens often use money to show off how much they care for someone. They use every birthday, holiday, and relationship milestone as an excuse to buy and exchange gifts. But how appropriate are these expressions of caring (love)? How much money is being spent? Are gifts even necessary? And what meaning do teens attach to gifts? Parents often overlook this aspect of teen dating, even though gift giving can cause as much stress and conflict in relationships as curfews and clothes. To keep gifts from giving your family grief, you have to set limits for what's appropriate for your teen to give to and accept from girlfriends and boyfriends. Following are some guidelines to discuss with your teen.

Gifts Should Not Be Too Intimate

Is it okay for your daughter to buy her guy boxers or briefs, or to accept a gift of lingerie from him? You might be surprised to know that many teens believe intimate gifts are no big deal. We spoke to one father who told us how he came home from work one afternoon and found a package at his front door. It was addressed to his 15-year-old son, and the mailing label suggested the package came from Victoria's Secret. The dad opened the box and found a red lace bra and matching panty inside. The dad hoped it was a shipping mistake, but when his son came home from school, he admitted to ordering the racy lingerie. Apparently, he wanted to give his 13-year-old girlfriend a special gift for her birthday. When Dad asked him how he got such an idea, the boy said that his friends had given similar gifts to their girlfriends and they liked it. He added that he'd seen so many billboards, movies, television shows, and people on the street wearing underwear as outerwear that he didn't think it was inappropriate.

Giving a gift of intimate apparel doesn't seem to faze girls either. One young lady told us she bought a pair of boxer shorts for her boyfriend because that's what he wanted for Christmas. However, when she told her mother about the gift, Mom responded, "He's not always going to get what he wants, now is he?" The mom then drove her daughter to the department store to return the boxer shorts, and, together, they shopped for a more modest gift (a t-shirt with the name of his favorite sports team).

Boxer shorts, bikini briefs, and bras are popular items with teens, perhaps because they are coming of age in an era where a sexual look and attitude are celebrated. They've watched Victoria's Secret fashion shows broadcast on network television. They've seen porn stars become spokespersons for mainstream products. They've embraced the fashions of hip hop artists (sagging pants and exposed boxers) and pop stars-turned-models (thigh-high skirts and stiletto heels). The bombardment of sexualized messages and imagery from marketers, music, MTV, and other media that target teens has lowered the bar that defines modesty. Nowhere is that more plainly visible than on the trendy t-shirts teens wear today. They're walking billboards with messages that are often explicitly sexual ("Porn Star") or deceptively so. Have you ever seen a young girl wearing a t-shirt with the words "Future MILF" across her chest? If you're not up to speed on pop culture euphemisms, you may not know that MILF is an acronym that stands for "Mother I'd Like to F---." How would you feel if your daughter was given that t-shirt by her boyfriend? If she wears it, what is she saying to him, and what is she saying about herself?

We've spoken to girls who received lingerie and other racy apparel from their boyfriends. Many of them felt such gifts were a guy's way of saying he wanted the relationship to be more sexual. More times than not, the girls were right. Giving lingerie or any intimate gift can be a nonverbal way of asking for sex. Accepting such a gift can be seen as a way of consenting to a more sexual relationship, whether that's really true or not. That's why we think sexually provocative gifts – apparel, games, calendars, etc. – are inappropriate, regardless of the intent. Some teens will say they give racy or irreverent gifts just to be goofy. But how do they know the person opening the gift will see it that way? Even if the intent is to be humorous, gifts like that can cause unnecessary misunderstandings. Plus, the "ha-ha" factor is never as great as teens think it will be.

The grandparent (or buddy) test

Telling your daughter that gifts of lingerie or underwear are inappropriate seems to be a straightforward and easy-to-understand rule. But beyond bras and boxers, what does "too intimate" mean? You and your daughter may have very different ideas. When it comes to giving a gift, we recommend using the Grandparent Test. When your daughter is looking at gifts for her significant other, she should ask herself how the thought of him opening the present in front of his grandparents makes her feel. If it makes her feel uncomfortable, embarrassed, or possibly ashamed, then the gift isn't appropriate. Of course, she may argue that grandparents are old fuddy-duddies who blush at anything, so their opinion shouldn't matter. Well, if the grandparents won't influence her decision, maybe the boyfriend's buddies will. Ask her how she would feel if he opened her gift in front of his friends. Would she be embarrassed or humiliated? Would her reputation take a beating? If so, then the gift isn't worth giving. These are the questions and potential consequences you want your daughter to consider before she hands any present to her beau.

When the roles are reversed, and your daughter receives a gift, the same general principle applies. She doesn't have to accept or keep any gift that makes her uncomfortable or she feels is inappropriate. A simple, "That was nice of you, but I can't accept this," is a polite way to turn down an unwelcome gift. If a guy won't accept that answer or tries to force the gift on her anyway, he's being disrespectful. Hopefully, your daughter will see that the relationship, like the gift, isn't worth having.

Guys tell us the whole gift-giving issue can be uncomfortable and confusing for them, too. They want to show they care about the relationship, but they don't always know how to express it. Many awkward gift exchanges could be avoided if teens were a little more honest and proactive. Before another holiday or birthday rolls around, encourage your daughter to talk about her expectations with whomever she's seeing. She should ask him if he expects, or even wants, a gift on his birthday or on a holiday. Maybe they'll agree that gifts aren't necessary. At the very least, your daughter can tell him that any gift of underwear or other inappropriate apparel is going over the top.

Gifts Should Not Cost a Fortune

If some gifts are inappropriate because they're too intimate, others are inappropriate because they're too decadent. The $80 DVD box set. The $70 cologne. The $50 long-stemmed roses. The $100 friendship bracelet. By themselves, these items may seem expensive, but not excessive. But what if your daughter bought all of these things in a matter of months – a $300 tab – because she just had to show her special someone how much she "valued" their friendship? Do you want her spending that much money on a guy? Do you want a guy spending that much money on her? If she spends $50 on a Christmas gift, will she up the ante for his birthday? Does the next gift have to be bigger and badder than the last? If your teen thinks she has to spend more – or expects a guy to spend more on her – to have or keep a relationship, where will the spiral of spending stop?

Perhaps no single day best reflects how money influences teen relationships than February 14, Valentine's Day. More than a few young people have told us those 24 hours are some of the most stressful they ever experience. Why? Because marketers, retailers, their peers, even their dating partners, have told them that the day cannot pass without some expression of love. Too often, that translates into "What can I buy that says 'I love you'?" For teens, that can mean bouquets of flowers, boxes of chocolates, overstuffed teddy bears, or some combination of the three. We got a first-hand look at the consumerism of teen romance when we visited a high school on Valentine's Day. Throughout the day, deliveries of flowers, candies, and heart-shaped packages flowed into the school office. Every hour, dozens of teens were called in to claim their gifts. In the hallways, the comments we overheard included:

- "He's so sweet! He gave me a glass bear filled with chocolate kisses... makes me want to kiss him!"
- "He must really love you!" (said by a girl admiring her friend's heart-shaped necklace)
- "I sent her a dozen roses, so I better get laid."

As disheartening as it is to see teens judge the value of their relationships by the material possessions they give and get, the motives behind the spending can be downright depressing. Take for example the boy who told his friends he wanted to "get laid." Do you think he told his girlfriend that's why he sent the flowers? Of course not! But he's hoping the roses say it for him. Girls who are showered with gifts can sometimes be blinded by all the "bling." They see the gifts as a confirmation of real love. And thinking they've found true love, they might relax their personal boundaries. They spend all their money on a true love. They spend all their time with a true love. They share all their secrets with a true love. They get sexually involved with a true love. Girls do things in the name of love that they would not normally do, and much of it can be physically and emotionally dangerous.

While some girls are inundated by gifts from admirers, others use their own buying power to find and/or express affection. They waste so much money buying gifts and entertaining guys, it looks like they are buying a guy's company. Sometimes, they are. Maybe these girls lack confidence or maybe they believe guys aren't interested in their physical appearance or personality. Whatever the reason, they think money is their only appeal. But that attitude is just as unhealthy as if they were the ones getting all the material attention. Anytime one person in a relationship spends all the money or gets all the gifts, there's a real possibility someone is getting abused or used. When the emotional and financial investment in a relationship isn't equal, someone is bound to get hurt.

Return to Sender

It was so difficult watching and trying to help my daughter handle a breakup with her boyfriend – a boy the whole family had liked. But we never anticipated the second blow – the day he callously showed up at our house to drop off a shoebox full of the small gifts she'd given to him during their year of dating. As I watched my daughter's tears start to flow again, I wondered why he couldn't have just quietly thrown them away.

– HEARTBROKEN MOM

Giving and receiving nice gifts can be an addictive cycle for teens. It makes them feel good in the moment, but that warm glow eventually fades. To recapture the feeling, they buy more, often bigger gifts. But where do they go from there? Teens can lose all sense of perspective when they mix feelings of love with money and possessions. To help keep your daughter grounded and realistic about the proper role of money and gift giving, ask questions that force her to think about tomorrow rather than just today:

- How are you going to feel if your boyfriend gives you an expensive gift and a week later, you're no longer together? Will you be willing to give that gift back?

- If your relationship ends, what are you going to do with all the gifts he's given you? Will you throw everything away because you don't want to be reminded of him?

- What if you give him a pricey gift and then you break up. Will you ask for the gift back? If you do, what happens if he doesn't want to give it to you?

- What gifts do you want him to have from you if you're no longer together? How are you going to feel if you gave him something very personal?

Gift Guidelines

Getting your daughter to see why some gifts carry a price that's not worth paying is important. And that's a message that everyone in the family should hear. As a parent, you can counter some of the materialism that defines much of modern life by setting an example for your children. Here are some practical steps you can take:

Encourage your teen to be "counter-pop-cultural."

By this, we mean encouraging your daughter to be independent, unique, and not a slave to materialism or every passing fad. If she spends most of her free time cruising the local mall, she's more susceptible to messages from marketers and retailers, and may end up spending excessively. Cut down her shopping time by getting her involved in activities that emphasize giving to others in the purest sense of the word – volunteering at a soup kitchen, visiting a nursing home, or working in an animal shelter. Any time your daughter doesn't "buy" into the idea that she has to spend money to show how much she cares for someone, applaud her.

Teach your teen how to manage money.

If your daughter has poor spending and saving habits, it may be because she has never learned how to manage money appropriately. The earlier she is held accountable for staying within a reasonable budget, the better her chances are of becoming a smart money manager. This is particularly important if she doesn't depend solely on your purse strings for spending cash. If she has money because of a job, an allowance, or gifts, you don't want to be too heavy-handed in dictating how she spends every dime. But you also don't want to be completely absent either. Some day she will be on her own, and she needs to know how to handle money and make responsible choices so she doesn't get trapped in credit card debt or fall victim to every financial scheme that comes along. You're still the parent, and you have a responsibility to make sure she's not spending too much or saving too little. A good way to begin any money-management lesson is to look at the future. Does she want to go to college? Does she want to have her own car? Does she want to move out on her own after high school? All of these things come with expenses, including tuition, insurance, and rent. If she wants certain things to happen, she has to make choices. She can either spend all her money on guys and jeopardize her future, or she can save wisely and work toward achieving her goals.

During your discussion, tell her you understand that sometimes she will want to give a gift to a boyfriend or someone she's seeing. That's okay. But instead of always running out to buy something new, encourage her to look at gifts that are less expensive but just as thoughtful. Here are a few ideas to share with your teen:

- Make homemade baked goodies (brownies, cookies, cupcakes, etc.).
- Burn a CD with songs from his favorite artists.
- Spend time together at free cultural events (Shakespeare in the Park, Jazz on the Square, etc.).
- Frame a favorite photo or picture.

Make gratitude a core family value.

Take time to stop and count your family's blessings. In the flood of material possessions that flows through our lives, we too often take them for granted and barely acknowledge them before we move on to wanting something new. From now on, when someone receives a gift or you purchase an item that will benefit the family or make life easier, pause and savor the moment. Emphasize how the family or individual will benefit rather than how much the item cost or what it looks like. Teach your children to express thanks verbally or by sending a note of appreciation to gift givers. Being grateful is an attitude you want your children to always carry.

Gifts Shouldn't Be Forced or Frequent

As a parent, you don't want to see your daughter coming home with all sorts of gifts from a guy, nor do you want to see her spending all her money on presents for him. But where is the line between showing gratitude and being gratuitous? Most teens will say that birthdays and holidays require a gift for or from a significant other. On the surface, that may seem reasonable. But what if your daughter begins a dating relationship with a guy two weeks before Christmas. Is she obligated to get him a gift? If a guy buys her a present for any reason, does she have to reciprocate? If he gives her four presents, can she give him just one or none? Does her gift have to be equal in effort and expense? These are the kinds of ambiguities that are difficult for teens to clarify but can easily cause hard feelings and lead to unnecessary excess.

> "The roses, the lovely notes, the dining and dancing are all welcome and splendid. But when the Godiva is gone, the gift of real love is having someone who'll go the distance with you. Someone who, when the wedding day limo breaks down, is willing to share a seat on the bus."
>
> – OPRAH WINFREY
> PRODUCER AND ACTRESS

We recommend that you sit down with your daughter and discuss as a family the situations in which she thinks it's necessary to give a gift, as well as when she thinks it's okay to accept one. Birthdays and holidays are a common response from teens, but we also hear many say that anniversaries are made for gift giving. Teens, especially girls, are notorious for remembering every relationship milestone. Whether it's the first time they spoke to their special someone or the first time they went on a date, they will mark that day on their calendars and in their hearts. It's not uncommon to see teens commemorate the occasion with gifts, whether it's been one year, six months, or even six weeks. If you have a sentimental teen, she may tell you that celebrating these milestones is important. If that's the case, you have to help her determine whether putting that kind of emphasis on a relationship is necessary. You may want to remind your daughter that most teen romances don't lead to marriage. If she treats a relationship like a marriage, she may be setting herself up for heartache when it inevitably ends. All the effort and expense that goes into remembering those special moments will seem wasted.

To some extent, the limits you set concerning gifts will depend on a variety of circumstances. These variables include:

Age. An older teen who earns her own money and acts responsibly may deserve greater freedom to make her own choices about gift giving than a younger adolescent who has little dating experience.

Length. An exclusive dating relationship that's gone on for a year or more should have different, yet still reasonable, expectations than one that's new or casual.

History. A teen's past behavior – impulsive, manipulative, materialistic, etc. – inside and outside of dating relationships should guide how restrictive your limits need to be.

All dating relationships evolve, making it difficult to have rules that always make sense. But all the dating rules and guidelines discussed in this book should never remain static. They need to be revisited and adapted based on the behaviors you're seeing and the experiences your teen is having.

Oftentimes with gift giving, teens get caught up in the excitement of their relationships and don't realize how much they're spending or why someone is splurging on them. Here are a few points to discuss with your daughter so she understands why limited gift giving is necessary:

You don't want to look desperate.

If your daughter thinks she has to spend money on a guy to keep his attention, she's probably getting played. Eventually, she and all her gifts will get discarded. Or, maybe she's using gifts to keep him emotionally invested in the relationship. Either way, someone is being manipulated. Tell your daughter she doesn't need to buy someone's affection because her value comes from the way she cares for and respects others. Having a boyfriend may be nice, but it's not worth sacrificing her values or sense of self.

You don't want to look superficial.

Dating is about acquiring new friendships and developing social skills. It's not about finding one more person who can give you things on birthdays and holidays. When gifts or presents are constantly being exchanged, they lose their significance and their meaning. Anytime relationships become more about possessions than the individuals, people are left unhappy and unfulfilled.

You don't want gifts to be forced.

If your daughter gives a boyfriend several presents on his birthday or on a holiday, he may feel compelled to do the same, whether he wants to or can afford to. Likewise, your daughter may feel so guilty or uncomfortable because of the many gifts she's received, she may feel forced to reciprocate. To have a balanced, healthy relationship, your daughter should avoid engaging in excessive behaviors or encouraging them in others.

Limiting how often (and how many) gifts your daughter gives or exchanges in a dating relationship has many benefits for her, emotionally, physically, and financially. One of the best things it does is keep the relationship from becoming too intense or exaggerated. Of course, you probably won't see or find out about every gift that your daughter gives or receives. That's why talking about this and other dating issues is so important. The more you develop a relationship with your daughter, the more likely she will be to come to you when she has concerns or feels confused. As a parent, it's important to listen, but you also need to keep your eyes open. If you notice new clothes, jewelry, perfume, or other items in her possession, ask where they came from. When it's her birthday, ask her if her boyfriend gave her a gift. If it's the boyfriend's birthday, ask her what, if anything, she plans to give him. When you see or hear something that troubles you, share your concerns with your daughter. Give her a chance to explain the situation before you express your opinion or jump to conclusions. She may not appreciate your intrusion into what she thinks is her private business. But tell her the reason you want to talk about this issue and why you have certain rules is because you love her. It's not about controlling her life; it's about keeping her safe.

The True Meaning of Gifts

Gifts have meaning. If they didn't, no one would take the time to search for, find, wrap, and deliver them. Teens who attach too much meaning to gifts have a tendency to spend more, give more, and make them more personal. Like any other dating issue, gifts should be about balance and moderation. They should never become the primary reason for being in a relationship. They should never be used to manipulate a relationship. They should never come with a hidden agenda. They should never bring undue stress on someone. They should never be given with the expectation of getting a gift in return. They should never be used as a way to get sexual favors. They should never become a distraction from what really matters in relationships – communication, friendship, and respect.

As parents, if we want our daughters to have healthy dating relationships, we have to realize that the gifts they're giving and receiving often reflect the emotional and physical boundaries that exist, or are absent, in their relationships. We need to remind our teens that gift giving should be an act of thoughtfulness and caring; something they choose to do, not something they feel forced to do.

See how a "Mall Scavenger Hunt" (page 190) can launch your family's discussion about gift giving.

Chapter 7

The Appeal and the Peril of Online Relationships

Find a local hottie. Totally Free!

View 1000s of photo profiles – 100% free dating site!

You can easily date any woman with this proven dating system.

An easy way to find true love.

Simply type the words "online teen dating" into a search engine and you will find countless Web sites luring young people with promises of lasting love, physical perfection, and real romance. With 21 million kids between the ages of 12 and 17 spending time online, it shouldn't come as any surprise that virtual hookups happen. But why are young people looking for acceptance and affection online? Do you want your daughter going to the computer to find her next boyfriend? In this chapter, we look at why some teens are drawn to cyber hookups, and why parents should be cautious, if not skeptical, of these so-called relationships.

The Appeal for Teens

For today's teenagers, the Internet has always been available and easily accessible. They're comfortable navigating in the digital age, and they're embracing all the possibilities that advanced technology gives them. Instant and global communication has destroyed the barriers of time and place, redefining how teens can develop and sustain their personal relationships. Teens can associate and communicate with anyone at anytime. This boundary-free environment is naturally enticing to teens and excites them for a variety of reasons:

The convenience

Navigating cyberspace is second nature for most teens, and one of the most popular tools they have mastered is instant messaging. Instant messaging allows them to carry on multiple conversations simultaneously in real-time, sort of like a party phone. Sitting alone or with friends at a computer, they can continue the day's social life that began at school, or carry on conversations with individuals they don't even know. Teens use instant messaging to gossip, to goof on each other, to make plans for the weekend, to do homework together, to ask others out on dates, and to end relationships. Some teens prefer to communicate on blogs (online journals) that allow them to post news about their day or life as quickly as their fingers can type. Their readers can post replies just as quickly. The communication tools that teens use online have an immediacy that is appealing. They also reflect how most teens want all the other aspects of their lives to be: fast and convenient.

The anonymity

Imagine the allure of being able to create a new persona. Teens can step outside the labels and reputations they've earned or have been saddled with by peers at their schools or in their communities. The geeky academic can create an online profile in which she describes herself as an athletic cheerleader. The shy tongue-tied loner can become a romantic wordsmith online. Hidden behind nondescript or incomprehensible screen names, anyone can pretend to be whomever he or she feels like at a particular moment. Age, gender, race, and social status are whatever the online user claims them to be. The very nature of the Internet, whether in chat rooms, on blogs, or through instant messaging, has emboldened young and old alike to be more outrageous, more suggestive, more blunt, more revealing, more truthful, and more deceptive than they ever could or would be in person. In one survey, 37 percent of youth who go online admitted to saying things that they would never say to someone in person.[1] A survey of bloggers found that 66 percent feel free to "write on anything and everything."[2] For some teens, anonymity allows them to momentarily suspend and alter the realities of their lives. For others, anonymity allows them to abandon their natural inhibitions.

The therapy

A trend in the last few years has seen some young people throw their private moments and thoughts of adolescence into the public domain. No more keeping a personal journal locked away from prying eyes. Now, they post their feelings, fears, dreams, and doubts in online journals that are accessible to anyone. They share details of their lives and their loves. Here is an excerpt from one 15-year-old girl's blog about her boyfriend. (Note how her description includes many of the potential problems we've already discussed, including equating love to a momentary feeling, spending significant time together, sharing intimate thoughts publicly, and having an exaggerated sense of the relationship):[3]

"...I have an amazing bf (I know, *you think I'm too young to love*) but this guy is so amazing...he is so perfect!! I mean, everything he does, it's just another reason why I love him. I feel like I fall in love with him every second that I am with him.....he makes me so happy.... We spend so much time together, it just feels like I know every thing about him. We've been dating, ((the 13th makes 7 months)), but those 7 months feel like my whole life. I feel like I've known him forever. ...I have never felt like this before and I know in my heart that there is no other way to explain this feeling—except for 'love'..."

While often sounding like no more than innocent chatter, these online confessionals, complete with pictures, act as a form of self-help for many. According to AOL's *Blog Trends Survey*, nearly 50 percent of bloggers say they blog as "a form of self-therapy." The same survey revealed that in times of stress and crisis, 31 percent of bloggers find comfort writing in their blog or reading the blogs of others who are dealing with similar circumstances. By comparison, 32 percent of those surveyed said they turned to family and friends for comfort.[4] Most bloggers don't know who eventually will read their rants, and they don't seem to care. Whether they're chronicling their rawest emotions or life's daily drudgeries, they enjoy the freedom to express themselves without having to endure the shocked, bemused, sad, indifferent, judgmental, or uncomfortable gaze of the reader.

The Pitfalls for Teens

When young people go online, they're in an environment where deceit is easy and privacy is an illusion. Most teens we talk with seem to understand this, in theory anyway. However, when they get caught up in the excitement of a situation or the rapid exchange of messages, many forget where they are. In chat rooms, they can inadvertently give out too much private information to a complete stranger. On blogs, they can post their entire profile (with pictures) or life story, making it possible for anyone to track them down. Using instant messaging, some send intimate messages, seemingly oblivious to the fact that they don't really know who's receiving the message or that it can be manipulated, copied, or forwarded. Adolescents who are looking for meaningful relationships in this virtual world often don't understand that there are risks.

Everyone has read or heard stories about how adult sexual predators, posing as teenagers in chat rooms or on blogs, ensnare their victims. Oftentimes, they succeed because the victims revealed too much personal information about where they live, go to school, or hang out. The victims were too trusting or were duped into believing they were chatting with someone like themselves. As disturbing as that problem is, most teens are more likely to get emotionally hurt and have their hearts broken by other teens who are jealous, vengeful, mean, or thoughtless. Hooking up online exposes teens to risks they may not be aware of. Even traditional dating relationships and friendships can be undermined by what is said and done online. When the purpose of dating is getting to know other people better, trying to start a relationship in cyberspace is problematic. The biggest disadvantages involve being misunderstood, getting played, and missing out on having real experiences.

Being misunderstood

It's estimated that as much as 85 percent of human communication is nonverbal. So, if your daughter is chatting online with a boyfriend, girlfriend, or stranger, she can miss much of what the other person is "saying": She can't hear voice inflections, nor can she see facial expressions and body gestures – all of which can drastically change the meaning behind the words. The possibility of misinterpreting what someone says, or having someone misread what you've written, is quite real. Here is the text of an actual online conversation between two girls who were involved in a love triangle. The girls only knew each other through instant messaging; they had never met each other when they had this exchange:

Katie: "god it sounds like matt had more fun with you than he ever does with me."

Elizabeth: "now that isn't true!!!!!!"

Katie: "he is gonna cheat… so I will have nothing to live for anymore… so im gonna just plan on killin myself sometime soon. I wish you weren't gonna let him cheat Elizabeth, its not fair to me… but I guess if you want to let him that's fine… ill just start planning on how its gonna end for me… I'm not good enuf 4 matt"

Elizabeth: "u r good enuf 4 him!"

Katie: "matt hates me, you hate me, and im going to kill myself and if you send this convo to him in an email like you did the last one… im going to kill myself right now"

Is Katie suicidal? Does Elizabeth really believe Katie has a broken heart, or is Elizabeth shrugging off her comments as the rants of a drama queen? Is Katie trying to manipulate Elizabeth so she won't see Matt anymore, or is she expressing her genuine feelings? Remember, these girls don't know each other except for the messages they've exchanged online. They can't see how the other is reacting to their comments. Who's to say Katie isn't laughing while pretending to be crying? Who's being real? What's really being said? In cyberspace, there's no way of knowing for sure.

This conversation illustrates how easy it can be to intentionally manipulate someone or unintentionally misunderstand someone online. Imagine trying to start or maintain a dating relationship when words on a screen are the only thing you have on which to make judgments about a person's true intentions.

Another troubling aspect we see when teens chat online is their lack of appropriate emotional boundaries and self-restraint. Sharing intimate secrets, personal stories, and even making threats and accusations occur with surprising frequency. Teens have an exaggerated sense of security sitting in front of their computer screens. It's amazing what they're willing to say when it doesn't have to be uttered aloud to someone's face.

Getting played

Hollywood siren Eva Gabor once said, "Love is a game that two can play and both win." Ironically, she found love (marriage) five times, and lost it five times (divorce). We're not exactly sure how she defined winning, but equating romance to a sport is an analogy many young people understand.

Unfortunately, some end up becoming unwitting players in a game of online "gotcha." In one survey, 26 percent of teens who use instant messaging admitted to pretending to be someone else when sending messages.[5] This statistic seems accurate based on what teens have told us. For example, one game teens play on each other involves hijacking someone's screen name. Pretending to be that person, the hijacker sends an instant message asking someone out on a date. If the target replies with a "Yes," the prankster either responds with a biting comment, such as "Get a clue... I'd never be seen with your [insert derogatory comment here]," or strings the person along by planning a date. When the special night comes, the victim gets stood up and whoever's screen name was stolen is made to look like a jerk.

Another instant messaging dirty trick involves baiting someone (the victim) into making comments about another person whom the victim doesn't realize is part of the conversation. This usually happens when a group of friends sit together at a computer and find someone they want to toy with. They start by sending him or her instant messages. The first contact is usually an innocent message to establish trust. Then the manipulation starts. Here is an example of how Leslie was conned into making a certain comment she would later regret:

> **Dominic (to Leslie):** "What up, Leslie. Can't remember the chapters we need to read for English class… any clue?"
>
> **Leslie:** "Hey… chapters 6 and 7"
>
> **Dominic:** "thanx… class is lame… can't wait for spring break… u going anywhere"
>
> **Leslie:** "no… just gonna chill"
>
> **Dominic:** "do you know my friend spence? peeps call him space… he's invitin people over to watch DVDs next weekend… you should come…"
>
> **Leslie:** "maybe… don't really know him… but I know he's got a cute butt"
>
> **Dominic:** "I'll tell him you said that"
>
> **Leslie:** "don't you dare!!!!!!! I would die!!!!!!!"

Of course Dominic didn't have to tell Spencer anything because Spencer and several other guys were sitting around Dominic's computer watching the conversation unfold. There was never going to be any party at Spencer's house; that was just the hook they used to get Leslie to talk about him. It worked. At school, Leslie soon learned she had been duped. She was the "butt" of jokes, and the target of nasty comments and stare-downs from Spencer's real-life girlfriend. The situation embarrassed Leslie and hurt her feelings. But in many ways she was fortunate. Imagine if she had said something even more sexually provocative? Leslie had enough self-confidence and perspective to know that this would eventually blow over. While hurtful, it wasn't humiliating. But other girls aren't so lucky. Sometimes these "jokes" are more extreme, where the victims get intimidated or bullied. Maybe the victim is made to believe someone popular is interested in a date with her, when he's not. Or maybe the conversation turns to the topic of sex, and the victim's words are edited or misrepresented to make her look like a slut. Victims get burned because they forget their comments are never really private, even when they type "for your eyes only." Or the victims are so vulnerable, they want to believe everything that they see or read online. But there is always a certain amount of vagueness inherent in online communication. Kids who are too trusting can get played.

Missing out

Teens who are painfully shy, socially unskilled, or socially ignored at school are naturally drawn to the Internet. They search for friendships and relationships online because it's easier than changing who they are or overcoming the stereotypes that others have about them. With electronic relationships, they enjoy a certain detachment. No one is going to laugh in their face. No one is going to ridicule how they talk. No one is going to reject them because of how they're dressed or the way that they act. For many of these teens, their motivation seems to come from all the negative things that they can avoid by finding companionship online. But they don't see all the good things they're missing out on when they avoid having real relationships. They're not sharing the experiences of a great concert, a great meal, or a great game when they go online. Everything is impersonal, and there is no human connection.

One of the biggest disadvantages for young people who prefer online relationships is that they never get a chance to develop their social skills. Too many kids are not learning or practicing the most basic of skills, such as how to introduce themselves (make eye contact, smile, and give a firm handshake). That skill simply cannot be replicated on a computer. In fact, most social skills cannot be learned sitting in front of a screen. Adolescence is a time when social skills need to be developed. Being socially graceful doesn't happen by turning on a switch. It requires effort and experience, the kind of experience that comes from having real relationships, not the faux friendships found online. Adults who lack social skills are at a disadvantage in employment opportunities as well as in personal relationships. That's why it's so important that kids don't become so dependent on the Internet, using it as an emotional blanket to pro-

> "Friendship is the hardest thing in the world to explain. It's not something you learn in school. But if you haven't learned the meaning of friendship, you really haven't learned anything."
>
> – MUHAMMAD ALI
> BOXING CHAMPION
> AND SPORTS LEGEND

tect them from any uncomfortable, difficult, or even painful human interaction. Difficult moments are a part of life, and kids need to learn how to react to, deal with, and accept them. If they never learn, how resilient or emotionally healthy will they be in adulthood?

A Plan for Parents

As you talk with your daughter about the role the Internet plays in relationships, a good question to go back to is this: What is the purpose of dating? Remember, dating is about socialization. It's an experience that should be helping your daughter learn more about herself, as well as helping her relate to other people. From that perspective, online dating does nothing to help her hone her social skills, teach her how to handle different social situations, or relate one-to-one with anyone. Cyberdating denies teens the very things they need the most.

We've had some single parents tell us that they use online dating services. A common concern they have is how to tell their daughters it's a bad idea when they themselves use these services. Aren't they being hypocritical? No, they're not. Online dating services have been wonderful outlets for divorced, widowed, and single adults to meet new people and find new relationships. But most adults are responsible, mature, and cautious enough to understand the environment they're in. Most dating sites encourage their members to start a relationship by exchanging instant messages or e-mails that are not too personal. As two people become more comfortable, they might exchange phone numbers and have several conversations before they ever agree to meet in per-

Opinions about Online Activities

A survey of parents and teens conducted by the Pew Internet and American Life Project in 2005 found:

- 81% of parents of teens who go online say that teens aren't careful enough when giving out personal information on the Internet.
- 79% of teens who go online agree that teens aren't careful enough when sharing personal information online.
- 65% of parents and 64% of teens say that teens do things online that they wouldn't want their parents to know about.

Source: Pew Internet and American Life Project. (2005). Protecting Teens Online [Online]. Available: www.pewinternet.org/PPF/r/152/report_display.asp.

son. And if they decide to meet, they don't rendezvous in a deserted parking lot. They agree to meet each other in a public place at a public event, and they tell others what their plan is. Most adults have the maturity and the skills to handle themselves. If your daughter challenges your use of online dating services, simply tell her you're capable of making smart choices and appropriate decisions. As an adult, you possess the experience and the skills to stay physically and emotionally safe.

If you think your daughter is the kind of person who would be drawn to cyberdating, or you think she has become too dependent on Internet relationships, help her expand her social opportunities. Encourage her to join school, civic, church, art, or sports clubs. Help your daughter learn skills for meeting and talking with peers (and adults) face-to-face. Increase her comfort level for social interactions so she doesn't feel she needs the Internet. Provide her with opportunities to get real-life experience meeting people, having conversations, and developing friendships. The more comfortable she becomes around people, the less likely she will be to go online in search of companionship.

Teach Online Etiquette

A survey by the Pew Internet and American Life Project found that slightly more than half of parents with teenage girls ages 15 to 17 say they monitor their daughters' online activities.[6] What do the other half do? In our experience, much of what kids say and do on the Internet is done without the knowledge or supervision of Mom and Dad. That's unfortunate. The convenience, speed, and false sense of intimacy that attracts teens to cyberspace can also punish them. The process of trying to connect with people while still feeling somewhat disconnected from them can create situations where teens express themselves without thought or restraint. As a parent, you might not be able to control everything your daughter does online, but you can certainly set some guidelines. If you haven't talked about acceptable online behavior, now would be a good time to discuss your expectations and how they relate to her dating relationships.

Instant messaging

As we said, a popular way for teens to communicate with others in cyberspace is through instant messaging. This tool allows users to create "buddy lists" or contact lists that contain the screen names of others whom they want to stay in touch with, usually friends and family. However, it's not unusual for teens to have buddy lists with screen names of people they've never met or simply don't know. Some instant messaging programs have space for up to 200 names. Even for the socially connected teen, that seems excessive. Ask your daughter to identify the people behind each screen name. If she doesn't know who someone is, have her delete the name from the list. If she says it's a friend of a friend whom she's never met, have her remove the name. Instant messaging is like inviting people into your home. You should at least know who's being asked inside.

While it's important that your daughter knows whom she's communicating with, it's perhaps more important to set limits on what she says. For example, she shouldn't be using profanity, making threats or mean comments, or asking inappropriate personal questions. In Chapter 6 we talked about the Grandparent Test. You can apply it to the language your daughter uses online. If she would be too embarrassed or ashamed to say something in front of a grandparent, then she shouldn't say it on the Internet. Make sure your daughter also knows that she shouldn't be giving out personal information about herself or the family – last name, phone numbers, passwords, credit card numbers, addresses, etc.

In terms of dating relationships, instant messaging should not be used to ask someone out or to break up with someone. Your daughter should never accept a date online because she can't be sure who sent the message, or if the person's being serious. She might be getting played. If someone wants to ask your daughter for a date, she and you should want him to have enough social skills to be able to do it face-to-face. Likewise, your daughter shouldn't be asking guys out online either. She can't be sure who actually receives the message or if the answer is genuine. The best conversations to have on the Internet are superficial ones. It's not an environment where deep, intimate thoughts and feelings should be shared. Once a relationship is established, then using e-mail and instant messages to make plans for the weekend or talk about the big dance are okay. There's far less chance your daughter will be getting played or misunderstood when a personal relationship exists.

When it comes to breaking up, doing it with an instant message looks mean and cowardly. Of course, your daughter can't control how someone ends a relationship with her. But if she's the one calling it quits, she should try to do it gracefully. Remember, dating relationships should have some element of friendship. If she wants to continue the friendship without the dating element, then she needs to show the boy some respect. Sending him an electronic notice that's it's over is anything but respectful. (We'll talk more about how to end a dating relationship without destroying the friendship in Chapter 8.)

Earlier we mentioned how instant messaging is often used by teens to pull pranks and become sexually aggressive or abusive. Let your daughter know that you're watching her online activities, including her instant messages. If necessary, invest in software programs that allow you to track and print out electronic communications word for word (visit www.getnetwise.org for more information). If your daughter knows you're checking up on the Web sites she visits, as well as who she chats with, she'll be less likely to act irresponsibly. And if you do see something that's troubling, you can intervene before things escalate out of control.

Blogging

All the do's and don'ts of instant messaging apply to blogs. Posting personal information, including phone numbers, addresses, even pictures, is potentially dangerous because it's impossible for the blogger to control who eventually sees or reads his or her site. In browsing popular blogging sites, like Facebook, MySpace, and LiveJournal, it's obvious that many young people don't realize or simply don't care that their postings are part of the public record. Maybe they're trying to be funny or maybe they want to push the boundaries, but some are posting sexist comments or sexually explicit materials, or bragging about their illegal activities. If all that weren't bad enough, some blogs seem to be exercises in character assassination.

Anytime a dating relationship ends, it can be painful. Imagine having your heartbreak being fodder for public consumption in an online diary. Young people also are using their blogs to flaunt their new dating relationships as well as trash their old ones. We met a girl who was still reeling from a bad breakup more than a year later because of what her ex did on his blog. He didn't tell her the relationship was over. Instead, he removed all her photos from his blog and replaced them with photos of his new sweetie. As hurtful as that was, the broken-hearted girl was embarrassed because all of their friends could read about the breakup and how much he was enjoying his new relationship. When kids are mad, want revenge, or simply want to be mean, they can say and reveal things that they often regret later.

Ask your daughter if she keeps an online journal. If she does, ask to see it. Remind her that any kind of diary she keeps is an extension of herself and that it should be private; online journals are not. She also should not be trashing anyone on her blog, nor should she be associating with groups that promote raunchy, illegal, or hateful activities. Explain the dangers that exist if she goes to the computer when she's mad. If she blogs when she's upset, she could easily say or reveal information that could come back to hurt her. Nasty or unflattering comments about past relationships should be off limits. Your daughter might complain that you're trying to edit or censor her feelings. Don't back down when she claims you are invading her privacy. There's nothing private about online journals. You have every right to protect her, and if

Can Your Blog Give You a Black Mark?

Facebook, the online directory, or social network, that is hugely popular on college campuses as well as in high schools, is not just for coeds looking to make connections. According to an online article from the *Des Moines Register*, university officials are using the directory to track student behavior. Students with questionable or incriminating postings (pictures showing drug or alcohol use in dorm rooms) are being charged with violations. A law enforcement official acknowledged that information posted on sites like Facebook "could be used to corroborate other evidence about criminal behavior." Students worried about their future employment opportunities may need to be more cautious when they blog, too. Employers may be going online to search for information about potential candidates. One recruiter had this to say about what people post on the Web: "Blogs are great things. They are also public information. It's very important to consider in this information age: Your private life can be public very easily."

Source: Erin Jordan, "Online postings could hurt students searching for work," Des Moines Register online, January, 22, 2006.

she's revealing too much online, she's putting herself in a vulnerable position. If she wants to express herself, she can buy a diary and write her emotions down on paper. She won't have any regrets if she keeps her deepest thoughts to herself.

Chat rooms

Ambiguity and deception are rampant in chat rooms. Most online sexual predators hang out in chat rooms that attract young people, such as fashion forums and sports forums. For this reason, and the fact that no one in a chat room can ever know if he or she is talking to a 15-year-old girl or a 50-year-old man, chat rooms are the least safe form of online communication. In fact, they can be so dangerous an officer from the Nebraska State Patrol's Internet Crimes Against Children Unit told us, "Nothing good happens in chat rooms, and kids don't need to be there."

Deciding whether or not it's acceptable for your children to go into chat rooms is a decision your family will have to make. We strongly suggest that if you let your kids visit chat rooms, that you monitor their conversations. And under no circumstances should your children pass along personal details about their lives with anyone in a chat room. Nor should they add that person's name to their instant message buddy list, or agree to meet anyone met in a chat room in person. The dangers far outweigh any potential rewards.

Final Thoughts

Your first instinct may be to remove your daughter completely from the Internet. Some days that may seem appealing, but it's not realistic or helpful. Technology provides wonderful learning opportunities and gives children access to information and virtual experiences that they may not otherwise enjoy. You don't want to inadvertently keep your daughter out of the social loop or cause her to be unnecessarily isolated or disadvantaged when she doesn't have to be. Technology, like most things, is as good or as bad as the user makes it. If you monitor her activities (putting computers in common areas instead of her bedroom makes observation easier and more effective), set boundaries, and teach her how to act responsibly, she can have a rich and rewarding experience. If she has trouble meeting your expectations, remind her that the Internet and instant messages are conveniences and privileges, not necessities, and they can be taken away if misused.

Finally, remind and teach your daughter that the most rewarding relationships are ones we experience with real people. Computer relationships cannot and should not take the place of face-to-face, social, and personal friendships and dating relationships.

 Make negotiating rules for Internet use more collaborative and less confrontational by doing the "Safe-Internet Contract" exercise on page 192.

[1] Pew Internet and American Life Project. (2001). Teenage Life Online [Online]. Available: http://www.pewinternet.org/pdfs/PIP_Teens_Report.pdf.

[2] America Online. (2005). Blog Trends Survey [Online]. Available: http://media.timewarner.com/media/newmedia/cb_press_view.cfm?release_num=55254441.

3   Posted April 4, 2005, on LiveJournal, "I Love My Beau." www.live-journal.com/community/i_love_my_beau/.

4   America Online. (2005). Blog Trends Survey [Online]. Available: http://media.timewarner.com/media/newmedia/cb_press_view. cfm?release_num=55254441.

5   Pew Internet and American Life Project. (2001). Teenage Life Online [Online]. Available: http://www.pewinternet.org/pdfs/PIP_Teens_ Report.pdf.

6   Pew Internet and American Life Project. (2005). Protecting Teens Online [Online]. Available:http://www.pewinternet.org/pdfs/PIP_ Filters_Report.pdf.

Chapter 8

Breaking Up Is (not so) Hard to Do

"The hottest love has the coldest end."

— SOCRATES

If you've spent any time around a love-struck teen, you know how prophetic the Greek philosopher's words often are. As parents, we know that most adolescent romances are fleeting and that high school dating relationships won't last. Yet we mistakenly assume our daughters realize this too; their tear-stained pillows and sorrow-filled notes suggest otherwise.

At the beginning of a budding romance, teens aren't thinking about how it might end. They're living in the moment. If they think they've found true love, they can't even imagine life without their "soul mate." As a result, when the inevitable breakup does happen, some are completely blind-sided, leaving them distraught and depressed. Others mask their disappointment by trashing the relationship or making disparaging remarks about their exes. On the flip side, there are those who can say, "Okay," and move on. Some girls even manage to remain close friends with their former boyfriends. How teens respond to breakups depends somewhat on the role teens play in ending a dating relationship. There will be times when the decision to stop dating is mutual: no blame, no pain. But the more common scenario has one partner telling the other to kiss off. That's why the phrases "bad breakup" and "teen romance" are so synonymous.

As a parent, is there anything you can do to ease the drama and trauma of a breakup? Can you save your daughter from a broken heart when a boyfriend calls it quits? Can you keep her from stomping on the heart of another when she says, "It's so over!"? When it comes to breaking up, is there any good way to say goodbye?

Happy Endings

The manner in which teens start and sustain their dating relationships is a good predictor of how graciously or boorishly they will react to a breakup. For parents, that's a critical point to keep in mind. If you prepare your daughter for dating, have an awareness of her relationships, monitor her behavior, and deal with problems as they arise, the painful hysteria that sometimes surrounds a breakup can be minimized, if not completely avoided. Again, we go back to the idea of having "The Talk," which was introduced in Chapter 2. Having ongoing conversations about the purpose of dating and its proper role in your daughter's life can keep her grounded and emotionally healthy. In fact, all the talks, rules, and limits you have about dating can be the difference between her feeling merely sad and disappointed by a breakup and her feeling crushed and despondent. Let's revisit a few of the talking points discussed in previous chapters. Each can help to minimize the likelihood of a breakup turning into an emotional breakdown.

• You remind your daughter about her life's priorities. School, family, and personal growth should be her main concerns; boyfriends and dating are secondary to all three.

• You discuss the concept of "dateability," and explain that the best relationships are based on friendship, not material possessions, social status, or artificial symbols of attractiveness.

• You focus her expectations on the fundamentals of dating, such as how to have and be a good date. You point out the danger and futility of trying to find true love or a future life mate in high school.

• You stress balance and moderation over extravagance and decadence.

• You teach the value of modesty as it relates to behavior, appearance, and language.

• You talk about individual identity, letting your daughter know that having a boyfriend may be nice but it's not worth sacrificing her values or losing her sense of self.

The more discussions and ideas you share with your daughter about dating, the better her mindset will be when she enters a relationship. You want her to realize that in high school, dating shouldn't be so serious. She's not likely to walk down the aisle any time soon, let alone with her current boyfriend. The better she understands that teen dating relationships are not forever things, that they eventually end but that friendships can go on, the more resilient she will be. She won't let feelings of anger, bitterness, or sadness consume her. By talking to your daughter, monitoring behavior, and keeping expectations in check, you may spare her and yourself much unnecessary angst.

"Sorry, Babe, We're Through!"

At some point in your daughter's dating life, she is going to be the one who gets "dumped." That is when all the dating skills you've taught and guidelines you've set are tested. Hopefully, she's learned to have a realistic attitude about boyfriends and relationships. She may be saddened by the breakup, but she won't let herself fall to pieces. That's what you hope for. However, being dropped by a boyfriend can be an emotionally jarring experience no matter how much maturity or perspective your daughter has. That's why the breakup is a good time to reflect, teach, and learn. Too often, parents either leave their daughters alone or blurt out trite phrases such as "It'll be okay," "You're better off," or "He wasn't that special anyway." Words of comfort may be necessary, but it's more important that you have a real heart-to-heart discussion with your daughter to help her process her emotions and work through her feelings.

If you're surprised or taken aback by just how hurt or bitter your daughter is about losing a boyfriend, don't shy away from asking painful questions. If her emotions or demeanor are really out of character or exaggerated, there may be more to the breakup than you think. A few questions that can get to the heart of the matter include:

How did he break up with you?

Sometimes, it's how guys break off a relationship that hurts girls more than the fact that the relationship is over. Your daughter may feel betrayed because her ex broke up online using an instant message instead of talking to her. Maybe she read about the breakup on his blog. Maybe he told his friends before he said anything to her. Maybe he let her find out he was cheating. There are countless ways of telling someone it's over without ever having to actually say it or explain it. If your daughter feels jilted because of the callous way her boyfriend broke off the relationship, try to help her take more away from the experience than just anger. This is an opportunity to look at how she can handle future relationships. If she's the one who calls it quits with someone someday, does she want that person to feel as badly as she does now? Hopefully not. Talk about how the boyfriend could have handled the breakup differently. Ask her what she would have done. (We discuss how your daughter can break off a relationship without being mean or petty later in the chapter.) Let the pain she's feeling be a lesson for her on how NOT to break up with someone.

Did you think you loved him?

Did she fall for the guy, thinking he was the love of her life? Did she build up the relationship into something it never was or could be? If she thought it was true love, did she express that love with extravagant gifts or sexual intimacy? In our experience, the more physically intimate a relationship, the more emotionally distraught a girl is when it ends. That's not true in every case; sometimes girls respond dramatically for other reasons. But if your daughter has an exaggerated reaction that lasts for days following a breakup, you may need to ask her how sexual the relationship was. This may not be a question you're comfortable asking, and the answer may be one you don't want to hear. However, her response may explain her anguish. Sometimes, girls act out sexually in response to other issues going on in their lives. If your daughter's relationship was sexual and/or she can't overcome her depression and move on, counseling may be necessary and helpful. If your daughter had impossible or idealized expectations, explain why they were unrealistic by reminding her of the real purpose of dating. Emphasize the importance of having appropriate emotional and physical boundaries. Let her know that the next time a boyfriend says "goodbye," her pain won't be so severe if she hasn't sacrificed her feelings, her values, or her body for the sake of the relationship.

What can you do differently next time?

This question encourages your daughter to look at her relationship more objectively. Behaviors or problems sometimes get glossed over or ignored because of the excitement of having a boyfriend. When he's out of the picture, any excessive or inappropriate behaviors can be seen more clearly. It's also easier to see what went right. Being able to recognize the good and the bad may help your daughter avoid certain pitfalls in her next relationship. This question, while reflective, is also about the future. Wallowing in the sadness of a breakup or obsessing over a failed romance isn't healthy for anyone. This question reminds your daughter that she will have other boyfriends and dating experiences. Her life isn't over just because a relationship is. In fact, the lessons she takes away from one relationship only make her stronger and better prepared for the next.

Who else can be there for you?

When your daughter is hurting, you can't delegate your role as the parent. She needs you, and the support and love you give her is what will help her to overcome her grief. But you're not her only emotional lifeline, nor should you be. Her friends can be great medicine. They can be blunt, revealing truths about the relationship or the guy that your daughter could not, or didn't want to, see. When they say, "It's all right, you're going to be fine," it can mean more than if it comes from you. Best of all, their mere presence can be an emotional lift. Being surrounded by friends can be a joyous distraction, making it very difficult for your daughter to dwell on negative thoughts.

Because friends can soften the blow of a bad breakup, it's very important that you encourage your daughter to maintain her social network. If she dumps or ignores her friends for some guy, where will her support network be when he leaves? You don't want your daughter sitting home alone obsessing about what went wrong or what her ex is doing on a Saturday night. You want her to be out having fun and making new memories. When your daughter is able to maintain other friendships while dating, it's a sign that she has balance in her life. And the more balance she has, the healthier her attitude and outlook will be toward boyfriends and breakups.

"Dude, It's So Over!"

When your daughter decides a boyfriend or a dating relationship isn't working out anymore, how prepared is she to actually tell him it's over? If you don't want guys dumping your daughter like a piece of trash, then you shouldn't let your daughter treat them the same way. Unfortunately, some girls can be downright mean or vindictive in the way they break up with guys, and in how they interact with them afterwards.

We've met girls who simply decided they didn't want their boyfriends anymore, so they started giving them the

I'm Not Your Social Worker

I dated a guy who, during the course of our relationship, I discovered had an Internet porn addiction. He would bring up porn on his laptop when we would study together, and I found all kinds of sexual images on his computer. He also liked to drink, even though he was underage. It was all too icky for me, and I told him I didn't want to be around him anymore. He pleaded with me not to leave him. He said I was a positive influence, and he was becoming a better person because I was in his life. I told him my job wasn't to make his life better. As bad as that conversation was, later his mom called me. She literally asked me, "Are you sure you don't want to get back together, because his life is so much better with you?" I didn't know what to say. Luckily my parents were home, and I handed the phone to my mom. I'm not sure what kind of exchange the two of them had, but my ex-boyfriend and his mom never called again.

— Just a Teen, Not a Therapist

cold shoulder and not returning their calls. After a few un-comfortable interactions and awkward run-ins, the guys got the hint. In the end, the girls got what they wanted, but they sacrificed their reputations in the process. Their ugly demeanor and behavior made them look much less attrac-tive. Then there are girls who get angry because their boy-friends do something "wrong." Sometimes, it's something as trivial as forgetting an anniversary. When these girls fly off the handle and decide to break off the relationship, they let their emotions turn the moment into a public debacle. They call their boyfriends names, make accusations, spread rumors, and basically trash the boys' reputations. They be-have as if the meaner and more disrespectful they are, the more strength and self-worth they show. For these girls, to be respectful is to be weak. That's certainly a message that is reflected in youth culture, especially on some of the TV dating shows that are popular with teens. But that shouldn't be the message you want your daughter to buy into.

We haven't met very many parents who bother to talk to their daughters about how to break up with a boyfriend. Most parents don't think to ask their daughters or their sons, "How do you plan to end the relationship?" Perhaps if more parents did, much of the juvenile, vindictive, and embarrass-ing behaviors we see would disappear. Teens have a choice to make when they break up with someone. They can end the relationship with grace and honor, or they can be malicious and spiteful. The latter is often chosen by those who are up-set because their girlfriend or boyfriend acted stupidly or said mean things. If their dating partner was rude or being a jerk, they think they have a right to be disrespectful, too. As parents, we have to do a better job of teaching our children the value of being respectful, even when being disrespected. If your daughter is angry and wants to use a breakup (or has used one in the past) as a way to give her boyfriend a taste of his own medicine, do your best to convince her otherwise. Being spiteful may feel good in the moment, but moments fade and the consequences of spite can be costly:

Lost friendship

There's little chance your daughter can preserve any friendship with an ex if she treats him like an enemy. If she breaks up with him in a way that humiliates, embarrasses, or ridicules him, she shouldn't expect forgiveness later. Why would he want to maintain any type of relationship with someone who would treat him with such disdain? How can he trust that she won't turn on him again?

Lost social comfort and sense of ease

If your daughter dumps a guy who attends the same school or lives in the same community, she probably will see him again. He's not going to disappear from her life when he's in the same clubs, classrooms, or social circles that she's in. Running into an ex, even when the relationship ends smoothly, can be uncomfortable. But it will be unbearable if she turns the breakup into a name-calling, hate-spewing episode. There will be unnecessary tension whenever they're at the same event or in the same room. It will be painfully awkward for her, as well as for those around them. She will experience moments of dread in anticipation of their next unavoidable encounter. All of this unnecessary angst and discomfort will directly result from her choice to make the breakup more outrageous than gracious.

Lost reputation

If your daughter is hurt or angered by what she perceived to be her boyfriend's bad behavior, she may be tempted to stoop to his level. But taking the low road won't make her look very good, or feel any better. If she acts mean, ugly, or irrational, people's perceptions of her can change permanently – and not for the better. Does she want to be remembered as bitter, vindictive, cruel, or "nuts"? How will she feel in the future, at class reunions or other occasions, when she runs into an ex-boyfriend, their mutual friends, or his parents? Does she want her bad behavior to be the first thing they remember? Wouldn't she rather have them think of her as someone who was nice and caring?

These are just a few of the unintended consequences teens can face when they coldheartedly toss aside a dating partner. Many don't give any consideration to what else they might lose – the respect of others, their reputations, their dignity, and their friendships.

'How-To' Tips for Breaking Up

If you don't want your daughter to lose more than a boyfriend or dating partner following a breakup, include this question when talking with her about the relationship: "If things don't work out, how do you plan to end it?" If she doesn't know, or gives you a glib response that suggests she hasn't given it much thought or doesn't much care, use her indifference as a teaching opportunity. If she doesn't want to talk about this subject, at least make her listen to the concerns you have. Point out the negative consequences of a bad breakup, and what she might have to deal with if she doesn't care about anyone's feelings but her own. Get her to start thinking about how she can handle a breakup in a way that's both smart and safe. Ultimately, you want her to walk away from a relationship with her honor and dignity in tact. You also want her to avoid getting hurt emotionally and physically.

Maintaining self-respect

Breaking up with honor is a concept that many of the teens we work with have never considered. Most don't know how to translate that idea into action. When we talk to girls, we point out that behaviors such as screaming obscenities, spreading malicious rumors, or trashing a guy's reputation are shameful and unnecessary. They can get their point across without being crass or cruel. It's especially important for a girl to show respect if she wants to maintain a friendship after a breakup. Even if she doesn't want to remain friends, she still shouldn't degrade herself. Odds are, the guy won't just disappear, particularly if they met on the job, at school, or through friends.

Your daughter may not give much thought to how she will tell someone she wants out of a relationship. She may think that the words will just come to her in the moment. More than likely, however, she will fumble to find the right words because of the tension and stress of the situation. The best way for her to avoid saying or doing something regrettable is to have a plan for breaking the news, including what she will say. The language she uses can go a long way in determining how calm and composed everyone is in handling the breakup. One of the most tactful approaches she can take is to focus her comments on the relationship, rather than pointing out the other person's flaws. Here are a few examples:

- "Our relationship isn't working out for me right now. I want us to go back to being friends."
- "I think we make much better friends than we do a couple."
- "There's a lot going on in my life, and I can't give our relationship the attention it deserves. I still want us to be friends."
- "I feel like you're more committed to our relationship than I am. I'm not ready to be this serious, and I don't want to string you along and make you think that this is more than what it really is."

In a perfect world, every young man hearing those words would understand and not react as though his heart had been stomped on. Fortunately, in most cases, the more thoughtful a girl is in how she ends a relationship, the better everyone feels afterwards. Still, there are times when guys cannot believe or accept what they're hearing, no matter how respectfully or tactfully a girl tells them it's over. Some will beg and plead for a second chance. Some will make promises to "change." Some will walk away in a huff, muttering derogatory comments. A few will become overly dramatic, even aggressive, threatening themselves or others. Any discussion you have with your daughter about how she will break up with a boyfriend should include the possibility that he may react badly. If he does, what is her plan?

Staying safe

One disturbing reaction to a breakup that can catch girls off guard is when an ex simply won't let the relationship end. Through no fault of her own, a girl might be harassed or stalked by an obsessive ex-boyfriend. (This excessive or unwanted attention can happen during a relationship as well, when a boyfriend demands to know – or dictates – how his girlfriend spends her time and with whom.) Stalking behavior might involve leaving threatening or disturbing letters in a locker; calling repeatedly and hanging up or sending e-messages begging for reconciliation; or dropping by the girl's home uninvited and showing up unexpectedly wherever she goes. A stalker will do all of these things and more. Some even take their obsession to cyberspace (cyberstalking), creating Web sites devoted to their former girlfriends or relationships. All of this can leave victims feeling helpless and anxious.

Hopefully, your daughter will never find herself in this situation. However, it doesn't hurt to talk to her about safety issues. For example, what should she do and who should she tell if a guy simply refuses to go away? The National Center for Victims of Crime offers these suggestions to teens who are being harassed or stalked:

- Tell a parent, friend, school principal, or another trusted individual about your concerns.
- Let friends or family know when you feel afraid or need help.
- When going out, let others know where you're going and when you plan to return.
- Memorize phone numbers of people to contact or places to go in an emergency.
- Save any notes, letters, or other items a stalker sends, and, if necessary, involve law enforcement.

If you or your daughter are fearful about a young man's behavior, call the Girls and Boys Town National Hotline at 1-800-448-3000 to speak with a trained crisis counselor who can refer you to local victim assistance services in your area.

Thankfully, most teen breakups don't turn into stalking situations or become violent. But violence in relationships can and does happen. That's why it's important for your daughter to take some common-sense precautions when deciding when and where to announce a breakup, even if she has no reason to believe or fear that a young man will become physically or verbally aggressive. Here are some situations where it may not be a good idea for your daughter to break the bad news to a boyfriend:

- **When she's riding alone with him in a vehicle.** When he's cruising down the highway, she shouldn't lean in and say it's over. If he reacts angrily, he might start driving aggressively. If he gets emotional, he may get distracted. He could even pull to the side of the road and tell her to get out of his car, leaving her stranded. Ending a romantic relationship inside a moving vehicle is almost always a bad idea, regardless of one's age.

- **When he's under the influence.** Seeing him drunk or high may upset your daughter so much that she just wants to end it right there. But with his inhibitions lowered and his thinking clouded, his reaction might be completely unpredictable. And controlling the behavior of an inebriated individual is nearly impossible.

- **When they're alone together in a private place.**
  Breaking up with a guy in the basement of his home
  when his parents are not around is similar to being
  trapped in a moving vehicle. Who can help her if
  things go bad? Being alone or isolated puts her in a
  vulnerable position because she can't control the environment. And how is she going to leave or escape?
  If she needs him to give her a ride home, will he even
  be willing to do that? How safe will the drive be?

These are just a few examples of predicaments you
would think teens would know to avoid, yet they have happened. Don't assume your daughter will know when a moment is right, or when a moment is wrong. Ask her to identify places and situations that she thinks are safe. Explain
any pros or cons associated with each. Even if your daughter
is certain nothing will go wrong, there's no harm in being
cautious or anticipating the unexpected.

Our advice to teens is that breakups should be done
privately, but in public places. There's no need to make the
end of a relationship everyone's business. That's disrespectful and opens both partners up to derision and embarrassment. However, being discreet doesn't mean being isolated.
Encourage your daughter to tell you or a close friend when
and where she plans to break up with her boyfriend. Make
sure that she knows how important it is to have somebody –
a friend, a parent, even a stranger – nearby. It's far less likely
that her or the boy's behavior will escalate out of control if
they know someone might be watching or listening. And in
case one of them does become aggressive, confrontational,
or overly emotional, someone will be there to intervene and
provide help.

Abusive Boyfriends

In our "How-To" tips for breaking up, we outlined strategies appropriate for typical teen relationships – the ones that **do not** involve physical or emotional abuse. If your daughter is in a relationship that has signs of abuse, or she is being abused, she needs to get herself out of the situation. She doesn't owe her boyfriend any explanation. And she should never be left alone with him or see him again.

In our work with adolescent girls, we often have to explain how relationships can be abusive, even if there is no physical contact. Many think of abuse only in terms of getting slapped, punched, or kicked.

Sadly, dating violence has many more forms. We urge you to share with your daughter the warning signs that a relationship may turn violent. They include:

- When a boy pressures her immediately to make the relationship more serious or sexual.
- When a boyfriend becomes jealous and possessive, and thinks his actions are expressions of love.
- When a boyfriend controls all the decisions or tries to keep her away from friends or family.
- When a boyfriend is verbally or emotionally abusive; this could include swearing at her, manipulating her, spreading false rumors, and trying to make her feel guilty.
- When a boyfriend threatens physical violence.
- When a boyfriend has been abusive in a past relationship, or accepts and defends the use of violence by others.

Source: Facts for Teens: Teen Dating Violence, National Youth Violence Prevention Center, www.safeyouth.org.

CONVERSATION STARTER!

Ease into a discussion about failed relationships using the "Breakup Blues" activity on page 195.

Chapter 9

Dating Is About Choosing, Not Being Chosen

We began this book by encouraging you to start an ongoing dialogue in your family about dating. What does it mean? What is its purpose? What are its limits? What value does it have in your child's life? We want to conclude by encouraging you to have one more special talk with your daughter. This time, it's to deepen her understanding of how healthy relationships evolve.

When we talk to teens about relationships, we often ask them if they are familiar with the stages of healthy dating. Occasionally, a smart aleck will respond, "You mean like getting to first base, then second base?" No, that's not exactly the progression we mean. But personal boundaries do play a big part in every stage of healthy dating. As we said in the previous chapter, one only has to look at how a dating relationship began to know what kind of ending it likely will have. If your daughter jumps into a relationship and commits herself emotionally, physically, financially, or sexually before she really knows what she wants out of the experience or who her partner really is, she's set herself up for a cold and bitter end.

Dating is a process that starts with friendship. If you want your daughter to have meaningful and satisfying experiences, then she has to take her relationships one step at a time. We've identified seven stages that healthy dating relationships go through. Following this balanced, gradual approach can lead to very rewarding experiences. Share these seven steps with your daughter and explain the important lessons that can be learned from each:

Step 1...Same-Gender Friendships

Learning to be a real friend is the basis of all relationships. In same-sex friendships, your daughter learns and practices the same fundamental social skills with her girlfriends that she will use to develop successful relationships with the opposite sex. If your daughter has not learned how to be and have friends with other girls, her dating relationships with boys will be difficult. You may need to refocus her attention so she learns how to develop, create, and maintain healthy friendships with girls.

Step 2...Opposite-Gender Friends

These are platonic friendships that help your daughter learn how to appreciate boys. Your daughter may discover that she has more fun in school just being good friends with boys – hanging around and having fun in a group, without the pressure of hooking up or getting serious. In these friendships, she can learn a lot about boys and herself, and ultimately, about how to best communicate with, understand, and be friends with a future dating partner or spouse.

Step 3...Friendly Dating

Like Step 2, this is an important time for your daughter because it gives her a chance to meet many different people and enjoy different experiences. Friendly dating can happen in a group, on a double date, or on a single date. But it always implies that your daughter is getting to know and go out with

Miss Independent

I was horrified by my daughter's choice of a boyfriend during her sophomore year in high school. I remember her being very cagey when I questioned her about him. She was reluctant to share with me because she didn't want to tell me he was 19 (she was 15), and he had been held back a year in school. I was a nervous wreck every time my inexperienced daughter went out with this guy. I voiced my disapproval often, and for the first time in her life, my daughter started lying to me. It was a horrible year, as we fought constantly about the relationship. I kept praying that this was her "bad boy," the guy every rebellious girl is momentarily attracted to because he's everything Mom and Dad dislike. While I hoped she would tire of him soon, I made sure dating my daughter wouldn't be easy. I made her curfew earlier. I asked for a complete report on where they went, with whom, and what they did. I talked to my daughter about choices and consequences. Eventually, she came around and realized that he wasn't good for her. I'm so glad I kept talking to my daughter and that she started listening. She's married now to a wonderful man, and we are very close.

— Persistent, Thankful Mother

a variety of guys. Her options are wide open because she's not committing herself to any one person or to an exclusive dating relationship. For friendly dating to remain friendly – rather than becoming hot and heavy – your daughter and her dating partners must be able to maintain healthy emotional, physical, and sexual boundaries. We suggest she goes no further than holding hands or hugging when dating at this level. Maintaining clear boundaries on limited physical and sexual closeness can help your daughter develop important skills, such as saying and accepting "No," demonstrating sexual self-control, and respecting others' boundaries.

Step 4... Steady Friendly Dating

Steady friendly dating occurs when your daughter wants to get to know someone better and hang out with him more often. The temptation to become physically closer intensifies as her emotional connection grows stronger. However, she still needs to maintain appropriate personal boundaries. Your daughter has much more to learn, experience, and achieve in life, so she should not be thinking about marriage or treating the relationship as if it will end with a ring on her finger. She also doesn't want to get hurt physically or emotionally, or make a choice she will regret. Most teen couples who steady date in high school do **not** end up married. They break up. This tells us something very important about friendship and dating skills. If you can help your daughter keep the focus on friendship (Steps 1 – 3) and encourage her to hold firm to healthy physical, emotional, and sexual boundaries in all her relationships, she is much more likely to avoid the pain, loss, and embarrassment of a gut-wrenching breakup.

Step 5...Serious Steady Dating

This type of dating relationship is **not** healthy for any high school teen. Your daughter should not have this level of involvement with anyone now. When she is a mature adult, she may be ready for this stage of a dating relationship. This is when she will begin to examine the relationship through the lens of the lifetime commitment of marriage. This is the time when she may be asking herself questions about who she wants to build her future with:

- Is this the person I want for a husband?
- Do I really love him?
- Does he really love me?

Step 6...Engagement

At this stage, your daughter is planning to share her life with someone special. However, engagement is not the same as marriage. Many engagements break off before the wedding day. That's why it's important for a couple to con-

---

Great Dating Ideas That Put Aside or "Save" Sex

Go on a picnic	Play cards
Bake cookies	Perform volunteer work
Attend church activities	Plant a garden
Visit local museums	Attend sporting events
Go to the zoo	Take long walks
Take dancing lessons	Visit an amusement park

Intimate Relationships

Researcher Desmond Morris, in his book *Intimate Behavior*, identified 12 stages that people typically go through as they build an intimate relationship with someone of the opposite sex.

(Stages 1 through 5 are appropriate for teens who are dating or building a relationship with someone.)

1. Eye to Body – The first thing we notice about a person is his or her physical body.

2. Eye to Eye – As we get to know someone, we look him or her directly in the eye.

3. Voice to Voice – This is a crucial step! Conversation is a critical component in getting to know someone.

4. Hand to Hand – This is usually the first type of physical contact. This can include a simple handshake or holding hands on a date.

5. Arm to Shoulder – This is a more intimate form of touch. This can involve putting an arm around a date's shoulder or getting a pat on the back.

(Stages 6 through 8 involve physical closeness that is appropriate for mature young adults involved in long-term dating relationships.)

6. Arm to Waist – This type of contact is more physically intimate than Steps 4 and 5. Examples of this type of behavior include dancing slowly or hugging.

7. Face to Face – This step usually involves kissing.

tinue to maintain clear and firm boundaries. Discussions about finances, in-laws, conflict resolution, children, etc., should occur.

Step 7…Marriage

For most people, marriage is the ultimate goal of dating. If your daughter learns the proper skills and maintains appropriate boundaries throughout the dating process, she has an excellent chance of achieving a lasting, loving marriage.

8. Hand to Face – In our culture, we typically avoid having others touch our face unless it is done in moments of physical passion, such as kissing. This is a more intimate form of touch than Steps 6 or 7.

(Stages 9 through 12 are appropriate for adults in committed relationships such as marriage.)

9. Hand to Body (over clothes) – This begins a progression to significantly closer physical contact. It usually leads to sexual intimacy.

10. Touch Above the Waist (under clothes) – More physically and sexually intimate than Step 9.

11. Touching Below the Waist (under clothes) – This is extremely intimate, involving physical, sexual, and emotional responses and consequences.

12. Sexual Intercourse

Having a frank discussion with your teen about sex isn't always easy. But this discussion is a must if your teen is to have the information she needs to make good decisions and to understand what healthy relationships are all about. It is up to you to let your daughter know that she can come to you with questions and concerns, or to just talk, without worrying about being embarrassed. For a list of books and information sources on relationships and sexual health, please turn to pages 205-216.

Source: Morris, Desmund. *Intimate Behavior: A Zoologist's Classic Study of Human Intimacy*. New York: Kodansha America (1977).

Final Thoughts

Dating is an opportunity for self-discovery and forging new friendships. The whole experience is meant to be fun, so embrace this stage of your daughter's life – it doesn't last forever! Dating gives your daughter a chance to learn more about herself and the woman she wants to become. That shouldn't bore you, depress you, or burden you. Her journey should excite you, so be a part of it and have fun! When she leaves for college or moves out on her own, the golden window of influence you have to shape her attitudes about boys and relationships will begin closing. Don't let the moment slip away because of fear or indifference. Take advantage of your time together by teaching her how to value people and develop real relationships.

We've seen what happens when parents don't involve themselves in their teens' dating life, when they don't set any limits or offer any guidance. Their absence or silence leads to situations in which teens get confused, manipulated, or even abused. Oftentimes, those problems could have been avoided if parents had paid more attention and communicated more with their children. Don't tune out this part of your daughter's life, even if you think she doesn't want you to get involved. Most teens do want their parents' advice, and chances are your daughter wants to hear from you. The young people we've met and the studies we've seen all say the same thing: Teens wish they could have more open and honest conversations with their parents, especially about the big issues going on in their lives. Remember, no one loves your daughter like you do. No one cares about her well-being as much as you do. And no one knows her better than you. If you don't provide her with any direction or teach her about what friendship is, what real love means, or how to have respect for herself and others, who else is going to care enough to do it?

All of the ideas, rules, and questions we've encouraged you to think about and share with your daughter are based on the principle that relationships are built on a foundation of friendship. When it comes to relationships, and especially dating relationships, there are choices and decisions to be made long before your daughter ever meets that one special person. The better she knows and sticks to her values and boundaries, understands what makes for a good or a bad relationship, and demonstrates appropriate social skills, the better prepared she will be to have healthy friendships and dating experiences now and in the future.

All of this thought, discussion, and planning may not seem very romantic to your daughter or very realistic to you. But try to look at it this way – it is when you take the time and effort to develop a healthy relationship with appropriate and well-defined boundaries that a real and lasting romance can flourish.

 Remind your daughter and yourself about the true purpose of dating by doing the "Respecting One's Body and Beliefs" activity on page 198 and the "Fill-in-the-Blanks" exercise on page 202.

Chapter 10

Conversation Starters

As a parent, you know how it can sometimes be awkward to start a conversation with your teen about a subject that he or she may not want to discuss with you. It doesn't help when the subject also leaves you feeling a little ill at ease. For many families, dating and all of its related issues is a topic often met with silence. Throughout this book, we emphasized the importance of having ongoing conversations with your teen about dating relationships. We understand that this discussion will be hard for some families, especially if the issue has created tension in the past. However, we know that when parents are able to overcome their anxiety and talk to their children, they're very glad they did. Most discover it isn't nearly as scary or stressful as they had feared.

If you're unsure how to get the conversation ball rolling in your family, try any of the simple conversation starters described on the following pages. They are always well received by the young people we work with, and they can help you have an open and honest dialogue with your daughter. These activities work well because they create a nonthreatening and relaxed atmosphere. That's important if you're talking about a sensitive subject or an issue that your daughter may have struggled with in the past. Each activity relates to content discussed in previous chapters, including gift giving, boundaries, and attire. We hope that you will try all of the activities, but you may find that some are more appropriate for your daughter, depending on her age, maturity, and experience.

We hope you enjoy the time you spend together doing these exercises. They're easy and fun to do. They don't require a lot of planning or extra work. And best of all, they can help you learn more about your daughter, including her opinions and attitudes about dating, relationships, and love. At the end of each activity, we provide several talking points. Use these prompts to focus your discussion and to serve as a reminder of the lessons you want your daughter to take away from the exercise.

Initiating "The Talk"
An Ice-Breaker Activity

In Chapter 2, we introduced the idea of having a serious heart-to-heart conversation, or "The Talk," with your daughter about love and dating. We provided you with five essential questions to ask in order to learn what her feelings and thoughts are on these subjects. Those questions are repeated on the next page for easy reference.

The purpose of having "The Talk" is to come to a better mutual understanding of the purpose of dating in your family. But before you start peppering your daughter with question after question, we recommend you ease into the conversation so she (and you) can get relaxed and comfortable. One of the best ways to break the ice is to share a funny story. The story can come from anywhere: Mom or Dad share a personal dating experience, retell a story highlighted in this book, or use an example from the movies, television, or a novel.

If you use a story from our book, we suggest any of the following:

"Cute Canine or Killer Cujo" on page 7

"The Name Game" on page 38

"Get Your Motor Runnin'" on page 69

"The Pooch and the Pink Cake" on page 101

Feel free to embellish or add additional details if you want to make a story more personal or relevant to your daughter's age or experience. Once you've broken the ice by sharing a good laugh, you can start discussing these questions:

1. What does dating mean?
2. What is the purpose of dating?
3. What is love?
4. Who is dateable?
5. What expectations do you have about dating?

Talking Points

- Tell your daughter how you would answer these questions. Talk about the changes you've noticed in teen relationships today compared to when you were a teen. Admit what you like and don't like about how dating has changed.

- Encourage specificity. If your daughter says "nice" guys are dateable, ask her to explain what "nice" means to her.

- Tell your daughter that you will always be there for her, and she can come to you whenever she's feeling confused, hurt, or just needs a shoulder to lean on.

What's Your Golden Rule?
A Self-Reflection Exercise

This is another great activity for starting your first real discussion about dating and relationships. The whole goal of this exercise is to help your daughter start thinking about how she wants a boyfriend or a date to treat her. The lesson being taught is that the Golden Rule means acting toward others in the same way you want them to act toward you.

For this exercise, use a marker or pen to draw a line down the middle of a large sheet of paper. At the top of the sheet, on the left side of the line, write the heading "How I *want* to be treated by others." On the right side of the line, write the heading "How I *don't want* to be treated by others." Then have your daughter write down her thoughts and feelings for each area. Encourage her to be specific and descriptive, such as "I want people to smile at me," rather than using generic phrases, such as "I want them to be nice to me." You also can write down your own answers, from the perspective of how you want boys to treat your daughter and vice versa.

When the paper is full or there are several statements under each heading, point out to your daughter that she has just created her very own Golden Rule. Explain how she can build a good dating relationship if she engages in the behavior on her "want to be treated" list. Remind her that she can jeopardize her relationships and friendships if she uses the words or behaviors that are on her "don't want to be treated" list. Here is an example of what the Golden Rule Activity can look like:

How I *want* to be treated by others	How I *don't want* to be treated by others
I want people to smile at me.	I don't want people to call me names like "bitch" or "slut."
I like it when people give me compliments.	I'd hate for people to spread rumors and lies about me.
I want others to offer me encouragement.	I would never allow someone to hit me.

Talking Points

- Discuss any similarities between your daughter's expectations and the expectations you have for her. If there are differences, talk about them.

- Ask your daughter to describe how she might respond if someone disrespects or harms her. Talk about some of the consequences she might experience if she disrespects or hurts someone she's dating.

- Discuss different types of behaviors and attitudes that make it more likely that your daughter will be treated with respect. Remind her how she can use the family's dating rules to help her earn the respect she wants and deserves.

Are You Dateable?
A Social Skills Assessment Activity

This is a useful exercise when you're trying to determine if your daughter is really ready to start dating. You can do this activity in many different ways. For example, you can have your daughter rate herself (**Good, Fair,** or **Poor**) on how well she thinks she does each skill. Or you can have her rate a potential date on how well she thinks he demonstrates these skills. Or you can rate your daughter, and then have her rate you. (If you agree to let your child rate you, expect to hear some criticisms, but be willing to accept the feedback. Our kids watch us as much as we watch them, and they can be surprisingly insightful at times.)

We've included the behavioral steps for each skill so you and your teen can practice the ones she needs to improve on. All of these skills help lay the foundation for healthy friendships and dating relationships. Although there are many more skills than we've listed here, we did make sure we included the skills of problem-solving and decision-making. Teaching your daughter how to make good choices gives her the foundation for handling most dating situations, including deciding who to date, what to do on a date, and how to end a dating relationship.

Greeting Someone or Introducing Yourself

Look at the person. Smile.

Use a pleasant voice.

Offer a greeting. Say "Hi, my name is…."

Shake the person's hand.

When you leave, say "It was nice to meet you."

Choosing Appropriate Friends

Think of the qualities and interests you would look for in a friend.

Look at the strengths and weaknesses of potential friends.

Match the characteristics of potential friends with activities and interests you would share.

Avoid peers who are involved with drugs, alcohol, gangs, or breaking the law.

Accepting "No" for an Answer

Look at the person.

Say "Okay."

Stay calm.

If you disagree, ask later.

Accepting Consequences

Look at the person.

Say "Okay."

Don't argue.

If given instructions or suggestions on how to correct the situation, follow them.

Disagreeing Appropriately

Look at the person.

Use a pleasant voice.

Say "I understand how you feel."

Tell why you feel differently.

Give a reason.

Listen to the other person.

Resisting Peer Pressure

Look at the person.

Use a calm, assertive voice tone.

State clearly that you do not want to engage in an inappropriate activity.

Suggest an alternative activity. Give a reason.

If the person persists, continue to say "No."

If the peer will not accept your "No" answer, ask him or her to leave or remove yourself from the situation.

Saying "No" Effectively

Look at the person.

Use a clear, firm voice tone.

Say "No, I don't want…."

Request that the person leave you alone.

Remain calm, but serious.

If necessary, remove yourself from the situation.

Dealing with Rejection

Examine behaviors that may have led to being rejected.

Remain calm and relaxed.

Use a neutral tone of voice with the other person.

Possibly disagree appropriately or give appropriate criticism.

If rejection continues, remove yourself and engage in alternative activities.

Initiating a Conversation

Look at the person or people you are talking with or the person or people with whom you want to talk.

Wait until no one else is talking about another topic.

Use a calm, pleasant voice tone.

Ask a question of the other person or begin talking about a new conversation topic.

Make sure new conversation topics are about appropriate activities and will not offend other people.

Showing Respect

Obey a request to stop a negative behavior.

Refrain from teasing, threatening, or making fun of others.

Allow others to have their privacy.

Obtain permission before using another person's property.

Do not damage or vandalize public property.

Refrain from conning or persuading others into breaking rules.

Avoid acting obnoxiously in public.

Dress appropriately when in public.

Setting Appropriate Boundaries

Imagine a series of circles radiating out from you. Each represents a boundary.

Picture people you know or may encounter inside

one of the circles, depending on the level of closeness with which you and a person are comfortable.

Disclose personal information only to those in your closest boundaries.

Touch others only in ways that are appropriate to your boundaries. Also, respect the boundaries of others.

Showing Self-Control

Monitor your feelings and your verbal and nonverbal behavior.

Use relaxation strategies to manage stress.

Speak calmly, clearly, and specifically.

Accurately represent your feelings with well-chosen words.

Use language that will not offend others.

Expressing Feelings Appropriately

Remain calm and relaxed.

Look at the person you are talking to.

Describe the feelings you are currently having.

Avoid profanity and statements of blame.

Take responsibility for feelings you are having.

Thank the person for listening.

Controlling Your Emotions

Learn what situations cause you to lose control or make you angry.

Monitor the feelings you have in stressful situations.

Instruct yourself to breathe deeply and relax when stressful feelings begin to arise.

Use appropriate words to describe angry feelings so they can be expressed appropriately and calmly to others.

Praise yourself for controlling emotional outbursts.

Interacting Appropriately with Members of the Opposite Sex

Determine the appropriate level of closeness or boundary that fits the relationship, observing proper moral standards.

A boundary is an imaginary line that determines the amount of openness and sharing in a relationship.

In general, boundaries are intellectual, emotional, physical, and spiritual.

Avoid overly physical displays of affection.

Avoid jokes or language that are sexually oriented and that may make the other person uncomfortable.

Using Structured Problem-Solving (SODAS)

(This decision-making process is appropriate for older adolescents and teens.)

Define the problem Situation.

Generate two or more Options.

Look at each option's potential Disadvantages.

Look at each option's potential Advantages.

Decide on the best Solution.

Using Structured Problem-Solving (POP)
(This abbreviated decision-making process is better suited for younger children.)

Define the **Problem**.

Identify the **O**ptions.

Decide on the best **P**lan.

Talking Points

- Review with your daughter the ratings she gave herself on each skill. Ask her to explain why she believes she is "Good," "Fair," or "Poor" at a particular skill.

- Praise her on the skills she does well. Offer encouragement in skill areas that may need more development or practice.

- Ask her what skills she thinks are most important in dating situations. Tell her what skills you think are most important, then explain.

- Talk about ways in which you could help her practice or work on improving skill areas she rated "Fair" or "Poor."

- If she rated a potential date (or current boyfriend) on his social skills ability, have her explain her ratings. Discuss how his social skills can (or do) affect the relationship in ways that are good or bad.

Good Date? Bad Date?
Assessing Appropriate Behavior on Date Night

Use this exercise to define the kinds of activities or events you would like to see your daughter enjoy on date night. For example, good dates typically involve activities that are safe, healthy, and comfortable for teens. That means neither person is put or forced into a situation that is physically or emotionally threatening, illegal, or against their beliefs or morals.

This conversation starter is similar to the Golden Rule Activity on page 177. Take a marker or pen and draw a line down the middle of a large sheet of paper. At the top of the sheet, on the left side of the line, write the heading "Good Dates." On the right side of the line, write the heading "Bad Dates." Then, you and your daughter jot down your own thoughts about each area. When both columns are full, stop and discuss each other's responses. Here is what a Good Date/Bad Date sheet might look like:

Good Dates	Bad Dates
Being active – bowling, roller-blading, or playing miniature golf.	Repetitive stuff, like only going to the movies or always going out to dinner.
Unique experiences, like poetry readings, boat rides, or museums.	Going to underage drinking parties or doing drugs.
Fun community events that are free or cost less than $20.	Sneaking into bars, trespassing on private property, or driving recklessly – drag racing or car surfing.

Talking Points

- Identify any questionable ideas you see under either heading. (You may have to convince your daughter that just because she thinks a certain activity would be lame or boring, it doesn't necessarily mean it's a "bad" idea for a date.) If you and your daughter have disagreements about what is a good date or what is a bad date, talk it out. Let her know why you feel some activities or events are either inappropriate or appropriate.

- If your daughter has dated before, have her explain what she liked or didn't like about a date (what made her feel uncomfortable, embarrassed, bored, excited, etc.).

- Tell your daughter that you love and care for her, and you don't want to see her get hurt or hurt someone else.

- Talk about having an escape plan if a good date goes bad. Discuss possible warning signs that a situation is dangerous, how to get out of those situations, and who to call for help.

Do's and Don'ts of Dating Attire
A Fashionista Art Project

In Chapter 5, we discussed how bare skin and revealing fashions influence the behaviors, thoughts, and attitudes of today's young people. The trend in teen clothes, particularly for girls, is a sexually provocative style that can sometimes communicate an unintended message that girls are not prepared to handle. The purpose of this activity is to help your family establish some basic standards of dress that are appropriate for teen dating.

To do this activity, collect several fashion magazines and apparel catalogs that you and your daughter can cut up. Take a poster-size sheet of paper and write down different types of dates that your daughter may go on. For example, there are formal dates (prom or homecoming dances), informal dates (dinner or a movie), and laid-back dates (bowling or bike riding). For each type of date, write down the phrases "What to wear" and "What not to wear." It should look something like this:

Prom

What to wear   **What not to wear**

Bowling

What to wear   **What not to wear**

Cut or tear out pictures of clothes and accessories from the catalogs, and tape them under the heading that you think is most appropriate. Have your daughter do the same. When you're both finished, examine all the pictures and talk about each other's choices.

Talking Points

- Discuss any similarities you see between her decisions and yours. When you agree with a choice she's made, praise her. When you disagree, explain your concerns.

- Discuss any possible negative consequences of wearing the "wrong" outfit on a date. For example, what might happen if she wears a mini-skirt to go bowling?

- Talk about how expensive the clothes are. Ask her what she thinks is an appropriate amount of money to spend on formal wear, including accessories. Tell her how much you're willing to spend on a prom dress and why.

- Ask your daughter if a date (or boyfriend) has ever told her what to wear or what not to wear. If that has happened, ask her how she responded. Discuss whether or not it's ever okay for her to dress based on what a date, a boyfriend, or even a friend says.

The Mall Scavenger Hunt
A Test on Appropriate Gift Giving

In Chapter 6, we cautioned parents about the influence that gifts and money can have on teen dating relationships. Some young people buy intimate, decadent, or frequent gifts for their significant others, then expect the same in return. Much of this materialism results when teens try to manipulate their relationships or simply don't know how to say they "value" someone's friendship. This exercise can help measure your daughter's attitudes about money and gifts, as well as help her set limits on what's appropriate to give and to get.

The next time you go shopping with your daughter, set aside time to go on a scavenger hunt. On the first hunt, each of you should take 30 minutes and try to find five items you think would be good gift ideas for a boyfriend or someone your daughter is dating. Take a pen and paper (or Palm Pilot and stylus) to log the name, description, and price of each item (no one is buying anything, just identifying items you think are good gift ideas). When the 30 minutes are up, (even if you or your daughter haven't found five items), meet at an agreed upon location to rest and chat about what you found. Then go on a second scavenger hunt, but this time put restrictions on what you can pick – no gift can cost more than $20 and each one has to pass the Grandparent Test (appropriate enough to be opened in front of Grandma without anyone being embarrassed or feeling ashamed). When you're finished, meet to discuss what you found.

If time or patience is an issue, shorten the activity by looking for three items in 15 minutes or two items in 10 minutes. You could even do the second scavenger hunt on a different day. If window-shopping doesn't appeal to you, or your daughter won't play along, try this:

Ask your daughter to write down two lists. On the first list, have her include 10 gifts she could give someone that are free (not store bought). On the other, have her write down 10 gift ideas that would cost less than $25 and pass the Grandparent Test. At the same time, you should make two similar lists. When you're both finished, compare your ideas.

Talking Points

- Discuss any similarities between the gifts she found (or listed) and what you found (or listed). When you agree with an item she picked, praise her choice and decision-making ability. If an idea is particularly original, acknowledge her creativity.

- Talk about any gift ideas that concern you. Ask her to explain why she picked the item, then discuss some of the problems associated with giving such a gift.

- Talk about any differences you see between the types of gifts she chose when she had no restrictions and the kinds of gifts she picked when she had restrictions. Remind your daughter that gifts can be special, even if they're not the most expensive, provocative, or trendy.

- Discuss some of the problems that can arise in dating relationships if one partner gives too many gifts, spends too much money, or makes gifts too personal or intimate.

Electronic Etiquette
Creating a Safe-Internet Contract

In Chapter 7, we discussed the difficulties and dangers teens can face with online dating. Two major concerns are the lack of human interaction and the absence of opportunities for social-skill development. But there are other issues, too. Even if you're certain your daughter isn't cyberdating, she most likely is using the Internet to communicate with others via instant messaging, blogging, joining chat rooms, or creating personal pages on Web sites such as MySpace.com. Use this exercise to establish boundaries for appropriate and acceptable online behavior in your family.

A Safe-Internet Contract is a written agreement that spells out the rules, guidelines, and expectations a family has about Internet use in the home. To create one for your family, start by searching for examples. We suggest visiting this Web page: **www.kids.getnetwise.org/tools/toolscontracts**. You'll see a sample contract, as well as links to other examples on the Web. We also recommend talking to other parents or teachers for ideas. A good contract will include rules similar to these:

- I will not keep online secrets from my parents.

- I will never meet "in person" anyone I meet online, unless my parents say it's okay.

- I will not fill out any form online that asks for any information about my family or myself without first getting permission from my parents.

- I will not use vulgar language, threaten anyone (even

if I'm only kidding), bully anyone, or say bad things about people online.

- I will not become a member of any online dating service.

- I will not post personal or identifying information on any Web page.

- I will instant message and share my individual Web page only with people I know and trust and have met in person.

After you find several examples, share them with your daughter. Explain that you want to have a similar contract for your family and need her input. Write the contract as a family. Then have everyone sign it, and post it next to the computer. As you are writing, talk about potential consequences (losing computer time) for violating any part of the contract.

If you're unfamiliar with some of the technology or aren't sure how kids misuse, or are abused by, online communication, visit the Web sites listed below. They have great information for your kids, too.

www.stoptextbully.com

www.protectkids.com

www.getnetwise.org

Talking Points

- Ask your daughter if she's ever experienced an uncomfortable or embarrassing situation while online. Let her know that she can and should come to you if she feels threatened or harassed.

- Remind your daughter that chatting online is not a private, secure environment. Talk about any instances where she or someone she knows said something online that led to fights, tension, or embarrassment at school or among friends.

- Talk about what is or is not an appropriate topic of conversation when chatting online. Have her tell you 20 topics that she thinks are okay for her to talk about and 20 topics that she thinks she should never discuss with someone online. Have her explain her answers, and share your thoughts and concerns.

- Discuss the issue of cyberdating, including whether or not that type of relationship appeals to your daughter. If it does, find out what's so appealing to her. Share with her the disadvantages of online romances, and why you want her to focus on real relationships and friendships.

The Breakup Blues
An Exercise in Decision-Making

In Chapter 8, we looked at how and why teens can feel angry, bitter, and depressed following a breakup. Too often, a bad breakup involves displays of vindictive, juvenile, mean, or embarrassing behaviors that are completely unnecessary. The purpose of this activity is to help your daughter avoid such a situation (or to prevent a bad breakup from happening again).

If this topic is too depressing for your daughter or she simply isn't interested in talking to you, lighten the mood by injecting some music into your discussion. First, select a genre of music that you both enjoy, or at least can tolerate – rock, hip-hop, pop, country, Motown, rap – then pick a song with lyrics that describe a lost love or failed relationship. After listening to the song together, discuss its message and how it relates to your daughter's experiences or expectations.

As part of your discussion, do a problem-solving SODAS activity together. SODAS stands for Situation, Options, Disadvantages, Advantages, and Solution. It's a structured way of thinking through problems and making the best possible decision. SODAS is one of the social skills included in the *Are You Dateable?* activity and described on page 184. To start, have your daughter write down the problem or situation she faces. For example, she wants to break up with her boyfriend or she has been "dumped" by a boyfriend. Have her think of three or four options she has for dealing with the situation. Suggest options if she has trouble coming up with some. Then have her write down the disadvantages and advantages of each option. You may have to offer some advice if she has limited life experience and doesn't fully understand what the potential outcomes could be. Finally, let her choose the solution that she feels is most appropriate and discuss it. Here is what it might sound like:

Situation: I'm going to break up with my boyfriend.

Options: He's taking me to the school dance, so I can tell him there. Or, I'll send him an instant message. Or, I can talk to him privately at school.

Disadvantages: At the dance, friends might pressure me not to break up with him; it might ruin everyone's fun. He might ignore my instant message, or think I'm joking. At school, I probably won't be able to think about anything else during the day.

Advantages: At the dance, I won't feel guilty dancing with other guys. Sending an instant message means I won't have to see his reaction. At school, friends will be around to give me support and calm me down if necessary.

Solution: I think telling him privately at school is the best option.

Talking Points

- Discuss the different reasons people use to end dating relationships. Ask your daughter if some reasons are better than others. Ask her to explain.

- Talk about self-respect and friendship. Discuss how her reputation might suffer if she acts immature or is cruel during a breakup, and how that behavior might destroy any friendship.
- Discuss what she can do to maintain her honor and dignity when handling a difficult breakup, including how to stay emotionally and physically safe.

Respecting One's Body and Beliefs
An Exercise in Healthy Boundaries

Chapter 9 described the Seven Steps of Healthy Dating, along with the 12 Stages of Physical Closeness. For many teens, setting and maintaining healthy emotional, physical, and sexual boundaries is difficult. Too many young people leap frog the natural progression or steps of developing a healthy relationship in order to get to the "good stuff" first, and then regret it later. Use this exercise to gain insights into what your daughter believes are appropriate boundaries for relationships and to encourage an honest discussion about emotional, physical, and sexual intimacy.

If you are uncomfortable talking about intimacy, particularly as it relates to sexual behavior, don't rush into or force a conversation with your daughter. Try to prepare yourself first. Here are a few suggestions to boost your confidence and overcome your reluctance or discomfort:

- Seek advice from a counselor or other professional, perhaps a family physician.

- Read books on sexuality, or watch videotapes on ways to teach youth about sexual issues. (See our Recommended Reading list on page 209 and our Helpful Resources list on page 205.)

- Try to relax. Practice beforehand what you want to say to your daughter.

- Be honest about your discomfort: "It's hard for me to talk about this, but...."

- Approach the discussion with a sense of humor.

The more comfortable and straightforward you are, the less awkward it will be for your daughter. Always try to create an atmosphere that encourages honest, open discussions.

Before you start this exercise, review Chapter 9 and the information on the 12 Stages of Physical Closeness. When you're done, write down each stage (or behavior) of physical closeness on separate slips of paper. Shuffle the 12 slips together so they're in no particular order. On a large piece of paper, write down these three phrases:

Appropriate for teens who are dating or building a relationship with someone.

Appropriate for mature young adults involved in long-term dating relationships.

Appropriate for adults in committed relationships such as marriage.

Give your daughter the 12 slips of paper and ask her to read them. Then ask her to place them in the order she thinks the behaviors happen in a typical male-female relationship (what comes first, second, etc.). When she's done, have her match the behaviors to the three types of relationships described on the paper. After she's finished, discuss how she's grouped the behaviors and make any corrections using the following guide:

Stages 1 through 5 are appropriate for teens who are dating or building a relationship with someone.
Eye to Body; Eye to Eye; Voice to Voice; Hand to Hand; Arm to Shoulder

Stages 6 through 8 involve physical closeness that is appropriate for mature young adults involved in long-term dating relationships.

Arm to Waist; Face to Face; Hand to Face

Stages 9 through 12 are appropriate for adults in committed relationships such as marriage.

Hand to Body (over clothes); Touch Above the Waist (under clothes); Touching Below the Waist (under clothes); Sexual Intercourse

Talking Points

- Ask your daughter if she ordered the stages of physical closeness based on what she thought was appropriate or on what she thought you would say is appropriate. If she was trying to please you, ask her why she felt like she couldn't be honest with you. Tell her she shouldn't be afraid to share her opinions or feelings with you. If she doesn't agree with your opinion on what is appropriate behavior for relationships, talk it out. Explain any issues or problems that she may not have considered.

- Discuss how knowing about the 12 Stages of Physical Closeness can help her have better, more satisfying relationships.

- Talk about the consequences – physical, emotional, and sexual – that she will have to deal with if she sacrifices her body, her boundaries, or her beliefs for the sake of a boy who isn't going to be part of her life forever. If your daughter was in, or was hurt by, a past relationship that was too intimate, talk about what happened. Identify any actions or behaviors that created the situation, and discuss what she can do to avoid repeating a similar pattern of behavior.

- Discuss what your daughter can do or say to a dating partner so he understands exactly what her boundaries are, as well as what she can do if a guy tests her boundaries or pressures her for sexual favors. Remind your daughter that she, too, must respect the boundaries of others.

- Ask your daughter why she wants to date or have a boyfriend. Talk about what she hopes to learn from the experience. Share your own thoughts on what you hope she gains from having dating relationships. Remind your daughter that this part of her life should be fun. If it's not, then maybe her personal boundaries or expectations need to change.

Your Family Dating Policy
A Fill-in-the-Blanks Exercise

After reading this book and finishing most, if not all, of the discussion activities, you should be ready to formalize your family's dating policy. This written statement outlines the rules, limits, and expectations you have regarding your daughter's dating relationships. Whatever policy you draft, it should reflect your family's values and experiences. It should bring more sanity and less chaos to your home life. Ultimately, the policy should guide the choices and decisions your daughter makes in a more positive direction.

To do this exercise, you simply have to start talking to your daughter. You have to be willing to ask her about boys, relationships, and love. You have to find out what expectations she has. You have to discover what she already knows and what she still needs to learn. You have to hash out differences of opinion and find common ground so you can have a dating policy that is reasonable to her and acceptable to you.

When you have those conversations, you can start filling in the blanks to questions like these:

- What is our family's definition of dating, including its purpose?

- How can our daughter demonstrate to us she's mature enough to start group dating? Single dating? Car dating?

- Who is dateable, meaning what qualities should her dates have? How old should her dates be, or how much of an age difference can there be?

- How many dates can she go on in a week?
- What days – weekdays, school days, or weekends – can she go on a date?
- What curfew will she have?
- What kinds of activities/events are okay for a date?
- How far from home can she go?
- What is her safety plan if something goes wrong on a date?
- What attire is appropriate to wear on a date?
- What boundaries does she need to set so she stays emotionally and physically safe?
- How much money can she spend on a date?
- What consequences might she have to deal with if she disregards the family's dating policy?

Appendix A

Helpful Resources

The resources listed below provide additional information and material on teen relationships, including issues related to sexual health and dating violence. Listing these organizations does not imply that the authors agree with or endorse all of their materials or conclusions.

The Medical Institute for Sexual Health
1101 S. Capital of Texas Highway
Building B, Suite 100
Austin, TX 78746
1-512-328-6268
www.medinstitute.org

This nonprofit medical organization provides resources and information on many of the sexual health issues affecting today's young people, including teenage pregnancy and sexually transmitted diseases. It offers brochures, videos, and other materials designed to help individuals make good, informed choices about sex and adopt healthy behaviors.

Massachusetts Department of Education

350 Main Street
Malden, MA 02148-5023
1-781-338-3000
www.doe.mass.edu/hssss/tdv/polich.html

The Massachusetts Department of Education has been at the forefront in studying and addressing how schools can effectively respond and deal with violence in teen relationships. On this Web page is the department's sample written policy, "Updated Guidelines for Schools on Addressing Teen Dating Violence."

Parenting.org

www.parenting.org

This site contains information and advice from Girls and Boys Town parenting experts. Several articles on teen relationships are available, as well as articles on other child development issues. The content is appropriate for parents of toddlers or teens. A free parenting e-booklet, available in English and Spanish, can also be downloaded.

Girls and Boys Town National Hotline

1-800-448-3000
www.girlsandboystown.org/hotline/index.asp

Professional counselors can help you address any parenting crisis or concern 24 hours a day, seven days a week. The accredited crisis, referral, and resource hotline has assisted more than 7 million callers since 1989.

National Youth Violence Prevention Resource Center
P.O. Box 10809
Rockville, MD 20849-0809
1-866-SAFEYOUTH
(1-866-723-3968)
www.safeyouth.org

The U.S. Centers for Disease Control and Prevention, along with several other federal agencies, created this clearinghouse for information on prevention and intervention programs, publications, research, and statistics on violence committed by and against children and teens. Includes information to help young people avoid and escape harmful dating relationships.

WomensLaw.org
150 Court St., 2nd Floor
Brooklyn, NY 11201
www.womenslaw.org/teens.htm

WomensLaw is an online resource for women living with or trying to escape violent relationships. On this Web page is information specifically helpful to teens who may be dealing with dating violence. The site includes an "Am I Being Abused?" checklist to help teens assess their relationships, information on how to file a restraining or protective order, and state-by-state resources for domestic violence victims.

Choose Respect Campaign

www.chooserespect.org

1-866-723-3968

This campaign to promote healthy relationships and prevent dating violence is sponsored by the U.S. Centers for Disease Control and Prevention. The Web site offers numerous resources on dating abuse – fact sheets, posters, and brochures – for young teens, parents, and educators. Visitors to the site can watch a 13-minute video that spotlights teens who experienced or witnessed abusive relationships. An accompanying teacher's guide can be used for classroom or group discussion. There is also an interactive game (in English and Spanish) that allows players to create their own music videos while learning more about dating violence.

Appendix B

Recommended Reading

For Parents, Guardians, and Caregivers

Bailey, Beth L. *From Front Porch to Back Seat: Courtship in Twentieth-Century America.* Baltimore: The Johns Hopkins University Press (1989).

Bonacci, Mary Beth. *Real Love: Answers to Your Questions on Dating, Marriage and the Real Meaning of Sex.* Ignatius Press (1996).

Buddenberg, Laura and McGee, Kathleen. *Who's Raising Your Child: Battling the Marketers for Your Child's Heart and Soul.* Boys Town, NE: Boys Town Press (2004).

Cox, Melissa R. (Ed.). *Questions Kids Ask About Sex: Honest Answers for Every Age.* Grand Rapids, MI: Revell (2005).

Leman, Kevin and Flores Bell, Kathy. *A Chicken's Guide to Talking Turkey With Your Kids About Sex.* Grand Rapids, MI: Zondervan (2004).

Lewis, C.S. *The Four Loves.* New York: Harcourt Brace (1988).

McGee, Kathleen and Buddenberg, Laura. *Unmasking Sexual Con Games: Leader's Guide.* Boys Town, NE: Boys Town Press (2003).

Moir, Anne and Jessel, David. *Brain Sex: The Real Difference Between Men and Women.* New York: Carol Publishing Group (1991).

Shalit, Wendy. *A Return to Modesty: Discovering the Lost Virtue.* New York: Free Press (1999).

Strauch, Barbara. *The Primal Teen: What the New Discoveries About the Teenage Brain Tell Us About Our Kids.* New York: Doubleday (2003).

Recommended Reading for Adolescents

DiMarco, Hayley. *Sexy Girls: How Hot is Too Hot?* Grand Rapids, MI: Revell (2006).

Written from a Christian perspective, this book teaches girls how to create a style and image that is cute and cutting-edge but does not require squeezing into skimpy outfits, applying excessive makeup, or using provocative body art.

Herron, Ron and Peter, Val J. *What's Right for Me? Making Good Choices in Relationships.* Boys Town, NE: Boys Town Press (1998).

This book tackles the issues that make adolescence difficult, including jealousy, prejudice, anger, aggression, sex, bullies, and harassment. Through real-life stories, teens are given strategies for dealing with difficult situations and people, as well as how to take responsibility for their own behavior and future success.

Levy, Barrie. *In Love and In Danger: A Teen's Guide to Breaking Free of Abusive Relationships.* New York: Seal Press (2006).

In these pages, teens describe how their romantic relationships turned dangerous, and how they managed to break free from them. Honest and frank, this book offers important information to teens about physical, verbal, and sexual abuse.

Lookadoo, Justin and DiMarco, Haley. *Dateable: Are You? Are They?* Grand Rapids, MI: Fleming H. Revell (2003).

Written with an attitude and in a language that teens will understand and respond to, this book about sex and relationships addresses these issues, questions, and more: What does he say when you're not around? What does she really mean? What lies do girls and guys tell each other?

McGee, Kathleen and Buddenberg, Laura. *Unmasking Sexual Con Games: Teen's Guide.* Boys Town, NE: Boys Town Press (2003).

This book examines how young people can be conned and intimidated into sexual activity by emotional groomers, who are popularly referred to as "players." Teens are given advice on how to protect themselves by setting good boundaries, learning good friendship and dating skills, and recognizing when they are the target of someone else's "game."

Peter, Val J. and Dowd, Tom. *Boundaries: A Guide for Teens.* Boys Town, NE: Boys Town Press (2000).

Teens are encouraged to reflect on their lives and relationships in this book about physical, sexual, and emotional boundaries. Characteristics of healthy and unhealthy relationships are described, and stories are used to illustrate how personal space and feelings can be violated as well as respected. Its journal format allows teens to write down their own experiences when they felt their personal space, thoughts, emotions, or beliefs were challenged.

Appendix C
Recommended Viewing

If you're apprehensive about picking the right moment to start a discussion on love and relationships in your family, consider a night at the movies. Watching films, especially ones that touch on multiple themes and issues relevant to teen relationships, can lead to great discussions in your family. Here are a few we recommend:

Angus (PG-13)
A practical joke meant to embarrass the fat kid in high school takes an unexpected twist when he wins the heart of his beautiful classmate and gets revenge on the jock who tried to humiliate him.

A Walk to Remember (PG)
About this teenage love story that celebrates positive values and mutual respect, film critic Roger Ebert said, "After all of the vulgar crudities of the typical modern teenage movie, here is one that looks closely, pays attention, [and] sees that not all teenagers are as cretinous as Hollywood portrays them."

Ever After (PG)
This is a remake of the classic fairy tale Cinderella with modern twists, including a heroine with the beauty and the brains to rescue herself from hardships and find her prince.

Groundhog Day (PG)
In this romantic comedy, Bill Murray plays a boorish weatherman who, because of a supernatural twist of fate, is forced to live the same day (Groundhog's Day) over and over again. While stuck in this time warp, he realizes he has to change his behaviors and attitudes if he wants to have a meaningful relationship with a woman he likes.

Never Been Kissed (PG-13)
Drew Barrymore stars as a young journalist whose first assignment is to go undercover at a local high school to discover what modern teen life is about. Labeled a "geek" during her high school years, she's given a second chance to fit in and find romance.

Pride and Prejudice (PG)
Released in 2005, this acclaimed film is based on Jane Austen's novel about five sisters growing up in Georgian England whose lives are turned upside down when a wealthy young man and his best friend move into their neighborhood.

The Last of the Mohicans (R)
The brutal French and Indian War serves as the backdrop in this sweeping drama about love, honor, freedom, and survival.

The Princess Bride (PG)
Will the beautiful princess Buttercup live happily ever after with the boy she loves? This humorous fairy tale has enough surprises, laughs, and wit to keep moviegoers of any age entertained.

If you have a sentimental teen or you enjoy Old Hollywood moviemaking, we recommend these classic tales of love and romance:

> *Casablanca* (1942)
>
> *The African Queen* (1951)
>
> *Roman Holiday* (1953)
>
> *Sabrina* (1954)
>
> *West Side Story* (1961)

There are countless movies, television dramas, and novels targeted at teen audiences that deal with dating, love, and boundaries. Some of the most watched programs and widely read stories feature characters involved in relationships and situations that are deeply flawed or dysfunctional. It's quite likely your daughter is getting many mixed messages from media about what love is, what respect means, and what boundaries are appropriate for someone her age.

To provide a counterview or balance to the negative images and messages she sees and hears, talk to your daughter about values and character. When you watch a movie, reality show, sitcom, or drama together, ask questions to make her think more deeply about the issues presented and the relationships portrayed. Here are some questions you may want to ask your daughter when watching one of the recommended films or other entertainment programs you tune in to:

- How is love depicted?
- What's good and what's bad about the relationships being portrayed?

- Would you want someone to love or treat you in a similar way? Why or why not?

- Was anyone being victimized or taken advantage of? If so, how?

- How did the relationships between the characters evolve? Did any follow the Seven Stages of Healthy Dating or the 12 Steps of Physical Closeness? If they didn't, what kinds of problems resulted?

- How did the characters show respect, care, or concern for one another? Can you give specific examples?

We want to hear from you!

Do you have your own stories, humorous or not so funny, of dating dilemmas or disasters you or your daughter have encountered? As the parent of a teen daughter, do you have advice you want to share or concerns you'd like to see addressed? What about teen boys? Would you like to see a book about dating written for parents with a teen-aged son? What dating issues do boys and parents of boys have? Please send your stories or comments to the authors at one of the following addresses:

Email: NoSimpleRules@girlsandboystown.org

Mail: No Simple Rules
Boys Town Press
14100 Crawford St.
Boys Town, NE 68010